50
PLUS!

50
PLUS!
Critical Career Decisions
for the Rest of Your Life

ROBERT L. DILENSCHNEIDER

CITADEL PRESS
Kensington Publishing Corp.
www.kensingtonbooks.com

CITADEL PRESS BOOKS are published by

Kensington Publishing Corp.
850 Third Avenue
New York, NY 10022

All Kensington titles, imprints, and distributed lines are available at special quantity discounts for bulk purchases for sales promotions, premiums, fund-raising, educational, or institutional use. Special book excerpts or customized printings can also be created to fit specific needs. For details, write or phone the office of the Kensington special sales manager: Kensington Publishing Corp., 850 Third Avenue, New York, NY 10022, attn: Special Sales Department, phone 1-800-221-2647.

CITADEL PRESS is Reg. U.S. Pat. & TM Off.

First printing: July 2002

10 9 8 7 6 5 4 3 2 1

Printed in the United States of America

Library of Congress Control Number: 2001099104

Designed by Leonard Telesca

ISBN 0-8065-2312-3

*To **Geoffrey and Peter,** who one day will cross the fifty-year mark but whose ideas should be considered by all who are over this hurdle.*

Contents

Acknowledgments

A book is like a business: In the end, no matter how much time you spend working on it in the solitude of your room (or the confines of your computer screen), you cannot do it alone. Throughout this project, many people have helped me turn a concept into the object you hold in your hands.

My literary agent Reid Boates has once again proven himself to be a Most Valuable Player, not to mention an all-round great guy.

I interviewed many busy people who willingly shared their expertise with me. Among them are two of the hottest executive recruiters on earth: Gerald Roche, Senior Chairman of the international search firm Heidrick and Struggles, and Hobson Brown, Jr., President and CEO of Russell Reynolds Associates. They know pretty much everything there is to know about what it takes to get a good job these days, and their insights have been most helpful.

The same is true for Ted Feurey, a media training specialist who has worked with literally thousands of executives in fields ranging from aeropsace to pharmaceuticals. When he told me that "the worst mistake that people over fifty make is aiming low," I knew I'd found words to live by.

Charles Kadlec, an economist at J. & W. Seligman & Co., has been generous with his time and thoughtful in his explanations.

He is also a radical thinker. For a stimulating look ahead, be sure to read my interview with him on page 37.

Once again I want to acknowledge Carol Kinsey Goman, Ph.D., a widely recognized expert in managing change whose own career reveals a marvelous and unexpected trajectory. A writer and communications consultant to major businesses around the world, she has helped me clarify my thoughts on many occasions. (Check out her website at www.CKG.com).

Letitia Baldrige, the maven of executive manners, expresses her views with panache and has helped me formulate some of my own. She is also, like many of the other people I interviewed for this book, a role model for us all.

Bill Mitchell, Marvin Piland, and Susan Ratliff, my experts on image and style, have answered all my questions about fashion in the real world, where everybody wants to look good even if they don't happen to be undernourished nineteen-year-old supermodels with overstuffed wallets. They've also helped me in my personal quest to avoid the fashion police, and I am beholden to them.

Everyone I've dealt with at Kensington Publishing Corporation has been consistently supportive, not just of this book but of the others in the trilogy. In particular, I want to thank Bruce Bender, Bob Shuman, Tareth Mitch, Christine Lee, Kristine Noble, Joan Schulhafer, Michaela Hamilton, Laurie Parkin, Steven Zacharius, and Walter Zacharius.

Nancy Hathaway deserves a page of thanks and tribute of her own for her quality of contribution and personal assistance to me. She was a combination collaborator, editor, researcher, and master of what was needed at the moment.

Without my assistant Joan Avagliano. . . . well, I shudder to think. Her organizational abilities and clear-eyed intelligence have helped me create the career I wanted. This book, like so much else in my professional life, would not exist without her.

I also want to express my appreciation to my clients, both those who are named within the pages of this book and those who shall remain nameless. Many of them have opened their hearts and shared the nitty-gritty details of their careers with me. It is through their experiences, both the triumphs and the fumbles, that I have truly come to understand the process of creating a satisfying career.

Above all, I am indebted to my wife, Jan, and my sons, Geoffrey and Peter, for their patience during the time-consuming process of writing a book, their willingness to discuss the issues I've grappled with in it, and their all-around life force, which continually reminds me of what matters most. They sustain me. I am more grateful to them than I can say.

Introduction

I went to Canada the other day to meet with one of the top business people in the world. In the course of the conversation, which was contentious and difficult at times, I said to him, you know, I don't really have to do this. I don't have to spend time with you and go through this.

He said, I don't have to do this either.

We looked at each other and laughed, because it was obvious that these negotiations were important to both of us. So why were we doing it? I don't know if he ever came to grips with an answer. But I thought about it a lot. Ultimately I decided that I was involved in this particular transaction for four reasons:

- I was having fun
- I wanted to be involved in something that had meaning for other people
- I had to prove something to myself
- I wanted to show other people that I'm still in the game

It doesn't matter how old you are. Everyone has the same fundamental needs: to enjoy themselves, to be part of something larger than themselves, to confirm their own sense of their abilities, and to demonstrate to others that they've got what it takes.

And yet, there comes a moment, generally after one turns fifty—though in today's youth-obsessed culture, it can happen much earlier—when it becomes hard not to worry about being sidelined. My purpose in writing this book is to keep that from happening.

My Background

For my entire adult life, I've worked in public relations, first as an employee—and eventually CEO and president—of an established company, and later as the head of my own firm. In a classic case of public relations, you try to get people's stories in the press, you write speeches, you create booklets, you develop slide shows and film strips and PowerPoint demonstrations, and you present a person (or product) to the public.

We do all that and more. I've worked with hundreds of companies all over the world and I've counseled more than a thousand CEOs. I encourage them to think about their whole image, which includes how they present themselves, how they speak, how they absorb experience, and how they interact with their co-workers, their customers, their investors, and their families. Along the way, I've helped them navigate through crises that range from marital mayhem to nuclear meltdown (literally: I was an advisor during the Three Mile Island accident).

But I have noticed that nothing brings that look of fear into a client's eyes like facing the specter of aging. Even in their forties, and certainly by the time they hit their fifties, many of the people who seek my counsel worry that time has passed them by. I don't suppose they feel any better when I tell them that they only have one or two significant bites of the apple left.

My job is to help them take the largest, juiciest bite that they can possibly get their teeth around. To do that, I help them analyze what they want to do, what they realistically can do, and how they can make it happen. I do essentially the same thing with younger people. But younger people look to the future with enthusiasm. People my age—that is, folks over fifty—often look ahead with trepidation. And even when they understand the importance of repositioning themselves, they don't always know how to begin. As a public relations expert who has helped many, many people market themselves, I'd like to offer some assistance.

About This Book

Over the course of my career, I've come to understand why—and how—people succeed, and I've written about it at length. This book is the third in a trilogy that began with *The Critical 14 Years of Your Professional Life*. A lot of young people picked up that book and actually moved on the message. Literally thousands of them have written me, e-mailed me, and talked to me about the book and how they have applied it to their lives—even though it was clear from their questions that not all of them had read the whole book. Nonetheless, the experience was deeply rewarding.

With the second book, *The Critical Second Phase of Your Professional Life*, I found a more apprehensive set of readers. Midway through their careers, many of them were dissatisfied with their jobs, with their finances, with their social relationships. To put it plainly, they felt that they hadn't made it. They read the book because it offered real-world solutions to their growing anxieties.

When I came to write this book, I realized I was addressing a third audience. It includes people who are highly accomplished and economically secure, but intellectually bored or emotionally dissatisfied. It includes people who have lost their jobs (or can see the writing on the wall) and need to find new direction. It includes men and women who have a long-neglected dream that they're finally ready to pursue.

Most of all, this book is directed toward people who want another chance. They want to have their ticket punched one more time. They know they have something to give back, and they know there's something in them—an emptiness, an unsatisfied longing, a neglected talent—that remains to be fulfilled. These aren't people who are thinking about retirement, at least not in the traditional way. They haven't run out of gas, and they don't want their lives to become smaller or more constrained. On the contrary, they see the richness of life and want to participate. They have a spirit that longs to be kindled and made bigger.

I hope this book will help in that process. Let me assure you of this: It's not too late. If you go about it in the right way, the years after fifty can be the most satisfying time of your life.

But First, the Bad News

Leaf through the pages of *Vanity Fair* and ask yourself as you look at the ads, am I there? The answer is no. You're not there. It can make anyone over fifty feel invisible.

And that's not the half of it. Many people find, around the time they hit fifty or soon after, that the game changes. They feel less powerful, less attractive, and less relevant. Many of them worry about being perceived as over the hill, out of touch, or—at the very least—out of condition.

Speaking for myself, I know that my physical ability is not what it was. I'm not as fast as I used to be. And although I would like to tell you that my memory's as sharp as ever, that simply isn't the case. (Like everyone else my age, I'm hoping that these minor lapses do not signal early onset Alzheimer's.)

My energy and endurance have also declined. In my twenties, I could get up at dawn, exercise, work nonstop through the day, eat a huge lunch and a big dinner, fall into bed at one or two in the morning, and wake up refreshed the next day. Many years ago, I was in Elkhart, Indiana, for a meeting at Miles Laboratories, which makes Alka-Seltzer. Around eleven o'clock at night, my colleague Ed Dougherty and I left our client and were standing outside a Holiday Inn. Across a cornfield, we saw a sign blinking in the distance: Beer. Ed said, what do you say we cross the cornfield and get a couple of beers? It sounded like a great idea to me. We picked our way through the corn and, several hours later, closed the bar.

I would never do that today. I'd get the Alka-Seltzer instead. My days of closing bars and restaurants are over.

The Dawn of Awareness

In the last few years, I've picked up an unexpected habit. Like many other people my age, I find myself reading the obituaries regularly. In today's paper, for instance, they include a jazz musician, a Native American author, an environmental leader, and a British spy. Reading stories like those, I'm struck by what fascinating lives people lead. But lurking beneath such thoughts is an unspoken question: How much more time do I have?

The terrorist events of September 11, 2001, have only strengthened that feeling. It's not news that anything can happen to anyone at any time. But it's increasingly difficult to repress that knowledge now. Terrible things do happen.

And even in the best of all possible worlds, we're all vulnerable to the vicissitudes of age. As the Rolling Stones said—and I realize that reference dates me—"What a drag it is getting old."

The Silver Lining

Fortunately, aging has its compensations. The first is experience. In my own case, I interact on a daily basis with people in Washington, on Wall Street, and in the media. I've gotten to know thousands of highly accomplished people, not as masters of the universe, which many of them are, but as human beings saddled with unfulfilled wishes, insecurities, and the full gamut of emotion. My clients have shared the intimate details of their personal and professional lives with me. By allowing me to watch their struggles, they've helped me garner the expertise needed to deal with some very sophisticated problems. When new clients come to call on me now, it's because I can offer them that accumulated knowledge and experience.

Experience has also taught me that I don't need to rush. Many people want immediate answers. They want to get it done right now. That doesn't always work. Sometimes you need to mull a problem over and let your ideas germinate. When I was a young man, I was driven. Today, I'm willing to take the time I need to think more precisely, to focus more effectively, even to formulate my sentences more vividly. I wish I'd had that ability in my twenties and thirties.

Finally, experience has given me a number of skills that aren't directly related to my job but are certainly related to my overall level of success. Experience has taught me how to raise money on Wall Street; how to get the right lawyer; how to distinguish between people who claim to be experts and those who actually are; when it's crucial to seek out a second opinion (both in medicine and in business); how to distinguish between quality and schlock; and how to get a decent tailor. For a long time, I went to a tailor who sewed what they called a one-seam on my suits. If he'd double-sewn the seams, they would have been much stronger. I learned that the hard way.

I may be a hero to my clients. But I can assure you, no man is a hero to his tailor.

The Long View

If you've spent much time around people in their twenties, you know that even if they've taken Western Civilization or Global Studies, they are simply too young to have a solid sense of history. It takes a while to develop that. Fortunately, by the time they reach their fifties, most people have gained an historical perspective. If you're my age, you've seen trends and fads come and go. You've seen comedy move from Sid Caesar and Imogene Coca to David Letterman and *Saturday Night Live*—a very different kind of humor. If you were born in America, you've lived under twelve presidential administrations, half Democratic and half Republican. You've been through riots, assassinations, long lines at the gas pump, the Cold War, the Gulf War, the fall of the Berlin Wall, and the collapse of the Twin Towers. You know that the concerns of one era are not the concerns of the next.

Having that viewpoint is invaluable. Consider, for example, the economy. After a recession in the early 1990s, the market went gangbusters, unemployment declined, and a million dollars ceased to seem like serious money to a lot of people. A decade later, the bears lumbered out of hiding, the dot.coms disappeared like migrating birds, and the Nasdaq plummeted—to the astonishment of stricken, thirty-something top executives who had never experienced a down-turn before. As an article in the *New York Times* pointed out in May, 2001, whatever they were doing the last time around, whether they were still in school or just beginning their careers, they were not in upper management. It was not their responsibility to deal with these troubles. Now it is. To compound the problem, some companies, especially those created during the boom years of the Clinton administration, did not have a single employee old enough to have experienced significant inflation. Or to remember the panic of Black Monday, 1987.

I'm not saying that having been there in the bad old days necessarily makes it easier to cope with trying times. But it sure can help. I noticed, for instance, that after the terrorist attacks, young people by and large seemed more fearful than my contemporaries, who remember the Cuban Missile Crisis, the Vietnam War, and even World War Two.

Besides, as the philosopher George Santayana said, "Those who can't remember the past are condemned to repeat it."

Attitude Adjustment

It's easy to be a zealot when you're young. Early in life, everyone tends to harbor extreme views. I was probably guilty of that myself. Now that I've been around for over half a century, I take a more balanced view. I know that every stripe of opinion is out there and I understand, like other people my age, that if you can compromise, you can get a lot more done. We have to work in the environment we're in.

More and more, that environment is a global one. It requires being comfortable with people from every walk of life. After a lifetime of varied experience, it doesn't make any difference to me if I'm dealing with a Christian or a Muslim or a Jew, a Saudi or a Chinese, an American or a Canadian. It doesn't matter at all. I can even communicate with people who are intolerant, and believe me, there are plenty of them out there.

In my youth, I was certain that if I tried hard enough, I could convince people to see things my way and to act accordingly.

Today, that idea seems laughable. As a businessman and as a father, I have learned that you can try to influence people but you can't control them, and it's pointless to try. They'll surprise you every time.

I've learned to take it as it comes.

The Country of the Young

"Let me tell you about the very rich. They are different from you and me," wrote F. Scott Fitzgerald. "Yes," Hemingway replied in famous but apocryphal exchange. "They have more money."

In fact, we all know that wealthy people differ from the rest of humanity in a multitude of ways, not the least of which is attitude. The same principle can be applied to youth. The young are different from you and me—and not just because they have fewer birthday cakes under their belts.

The truth is, their interests and values are wildly different from ours. Their attention span is considerably shorter. Their heroes are often unknown to us. Most of all, they live and breathe technology in a way that is almost unimaginable to anyone old enough to have seen Stanley Kubrick's *2001* the first time around.

At the same time, young people have traits I admire, including their idealism. They tend to think that more things are possible than actually might be possible. I think that's great, because if you act on that assumption, you increase your odds of accomplishing something important.

I also think young people are more tolerant than we were. Older people are often hidebound by tradition. They're conscious of who is—and who isn't—a part of their social strata. Younger people don't do that. They have a broader sense of the world. In many ways, they're more at home in it than we ever were.

Besides, as you have no doubt observed, the older we get, the younger the people around us become. It's not just police and firemen and personal trainers who are starting to look like babies: after all, those are jobs for the young. Once you're over fifty, younger people may come to include your doctor, your dentist, your editor—even your supervisor. As an entrepreneur, I'm my own boss, so I haven't had to face that unsettling situation. I've certainly had younger clients, though, including many high-profile achievers who are obsessed about their age—even though they're significantly younger than I am.

The reality is that in a multi-generational world, getting along with young people is crucial. (I give the rules for that daunting task in Chapter 9.) It's true that 27 percent of the population of the United States is over fifty. That's 36 percent of all adults. In many ways we dominate the landscape. Even so, there are more of them than there are of us. It behooves us to understand them.

One essential aspect of that is staying current, and I'm not just talking about the news. Much as I am not thrilled with doing it, I watch television shows I wouldn't normally choose, I read the alternative press, I force myself to read articles I wouldn't normally read, and I listen to . . . Hootie and the Blowfish.

Do I prefer Frank Sinatra? Absolutely. He's a great singer. But I think it's vital to know what's happening now. On a personal level, it keeps the brain active and helps me communicate with my kids. On a business level, I've found that it's helpful because it plays back to people. If I'm making a speech or a presentation, and I can refer to a rap star such as Eminem (though he's hardly my favorite), I forge a connection with the young people in that group. Let's face it: Young people are unlikely to be up to speed on the singers of my youth. I'm the one who has to accommodate them. If my awareness of their cultural touchstones enables them to feel more comfortable with me, we both benefit.

No Threat

There's no point in going overboard, though. You can watch MTV all day long, pepper your speech with the latest slang, and run around in jeans so big a car could squeeze into them. No young person will ever mistake you for one of them.

Believe it or not, this is an advantage—assuming you accept the fact that competing with people who are decades younger than you are is ultimately a losing proposition. One advantage of being over fifty is that it doesn't threaten anybody. I'm not going to take anybody's job, step over anybody, or knock anybody out of the ring. I'm not dangerous. Young Turks don't have to fear me.

As a result, my observations and suggestions may take hold better, and they may feel more comfortable sharing information with me.

Age Is No Barrier

F. Scott Fitzgerald made another often quoted statement: "There are no second acts in American lives." Fortunately for us all, it simply isn't true.

Take, for example, Ronald Reagan. He was an appealing if ordinary actor who didn't even join the Republican Party until he was fifty-one years old. Four years later he was elected governor of California—and you know the rest.

Jimmy Carter was a peanut farmer who became president when he was fifty-two years old and was out of a job four years later. He retreated to Plains, Georgia—to nowhere, in the eyes of many—and proceeded to form Habitat for Humanity, one of the most successful, creative, hands-on charitable organizations on the face of the earth. A 1999 survey showed that, among retired people, he was the number one role model.

Harland Sanders is another example of someone who achieved great success right at the point when a lot of people decide to hang up the towel. He was running a gas station with a restaurant on the side when he noticed that his fried chicken was outstripping his gasoline in sales. He decided to franchise and, in so doing, created a phenomenon: Colonel Sanders' Kentucky Fried Chicken. He was in his sixties.

Gloria Steinem got married for the first time at age sixty-six.

Michelangelo painted the Sistine Chapel when he was in his seventies.

Brooke Astor wrote her first novel in her late eighties.

Admittedly, these people are extraordinary. But I can think of others just like them, people in their fifties, sixties, seventies, and eighties, who continued to interact with the world in a sophisticated, involved way. Some of these people remained in the same business—or even the same company—for years, but they shifted the focus of their activity.

Others launched new careers that were, in some cases, entirely out of sync with their previous accomplishments. For instance,

Jim Callahan left a job as city editor of the *Akron Beacon Journal* and became one of the top environmental public relations people in the country. But after several years, Jim decided that he'd had it. He stopped working, decided to pursue what had previously been little more than a hobby, and became a jazz musician. Soon he had gigs all over the country. This was something he loved but he'd never had the time to devote to it. Now he found the time. Did he make a fortune as a clarinet player? Not to my knowledge. But he played in clubs all over the country and he thoroughly enjoyed himself.

Other people have had a tougher time. They didn't walk away from their day jobs: they were thrown out. They suffered the devastating effects of humiliating failure—and they bounced back, even though they were old enough to be card-carrying members of the AARP.

Take a man I'll call Russell Perry. A top executive at a huge utility company, he was on vacation in Israel when his company faced an unexpected crisis. Maybe you remember it: the black-out of 1977. This was such a serious problem—not to mention a public relations nightmare—that his boss called and asked him to come home and deal with the situation. Russ was certain that his colleagues could handle it without him and he stayed on vacation. Big mistake. When he got back, his credibility in the company had fallen to zero. Within six months he was forced out.

As my wife will tell you, Russ talked to me every night for almost two years planning and strategizing how he was going to get back. Christmas, Thanksgiving, Easter, it didn't matter: we were on the phone. He never returned to Con Ed. After about twenty months of unemployment (and nightly phone calls), he landed a job, and a good one too—running a major organization in New York City. It was all a matter of how he prepared himself, how he positioned himself, how he thought about himself and his life, how he dealt with his family, how he conquered his fears (they were many), and how he marshaled his expenses. Although he had plenty of difficulties to overcome, both external and internal, he succeeded admirably—despite his age.

Here's a more recent example: I have a client I'll call Caroline Booth. When she came to see me, she'd been working for a large insurance company and she was over fifty and they just didn't want her. They did everything they could to drive her out and eventually they prevailed. It destroyed her. At first, she was too depressed to do anything other than file unemployment and discrimination claims. She felt cheated—and I don't blame her. She felt that they'd gone after her because of her age, because of her sex, and because she was a member of a minority. Needless to say, the company denied those charges. Her suit went nowhere. She was shattered.

But after about two years, she got rid of the emotional and mental baggage, pulled herself together, and started a business. I wish she could have done it sooner. Fortunately, she's a determined person who's extremely smart at what she does. I'm convinced that she'll succeed.

In the pages that follow, I'll discuss the new rules of business in the twenty-first century; the shifting economic landscape; the importance of image; the challenge of changing your life; how to look for and get a great job; how to go into business for yourself; how to become a consultant; the ten commandments of doing your own public relations; how to get along with younger people; and how to get back in the game. Along the way, I'll tell you how to activate your network; how to ask for help when you need it; how to improve your prospects socially, financially, and professionally; what to say in an interview; and more. In short, I hope to show you how to succeed—at any age.

I can tell you this: Age is no barrier to success. I know. I've seen people who are old enough to retire get new jobs, start their own businesses, forge new career paths, and fulfill the dreams of a lifetime. I've seen them go from despair to triumph, from complacency or boredom to full engagement in the wonders of life. And I will tell you: You *can* get there from here. This book tells you how.

1

The New Rules

Like everything else, business—and I'm using that term in the widest sense—has rules. To succeed, you've got to follow those rules, and that's true whether you're the CEO of a Fortune 500 company or a part-time instructor in a yoga studio. The confusing part is that, within my lifetime, the rules have changed.

The Old Rules

When I started out in the 1960s and 1970s, society was in flux but business was definitely not. It was an old boys' club with a rigid hierarchy. For instance, I was once flying on a corporate jet from Ohio to New York when one of the fellows on the plane opened up the bar and started offering everyone drinks. The CEO, who owned the plane, didn't hesitate to put him in his place. Don't you realize, he said, that I'm the one who opens the bar? The guy promptly sat back down.

In those days, business operated under a strict set of rules and assumptions. The fact that most of them were unwritten only made them more powerful.

A Policy of Exclusion

In many ways, the business world that I found as a young man was like a country club—the kind that a lot of people can't get into it. There was an unspoken rule that blacks don't apply. There was a rule that Jews don't get into commercial banks. There was a rule that women were secretaries—or they were home, where they supposedly belonged. Asians were strictly curiosities. As for Puerto Ricans, they were fictional characters out of *West Side Story*; in the real world of business, they didn't exist.

In short, the WASP—White Anglo-Saxon Protestant—ruled. And not just any WASP either. You had to be male. You had to be middle class or better. And you had to attend the right schools. I know. You might not think that someone like me—a white male from a middle class background—could feel the sting of discrimination. But I remember one time in the 1960s when I attended a meeting at a Midwestern bank. At lunch, someone suggested that we go around the table and tell everyone where we went to school. One banker said he was from Princeton, another went to Harvard, a third had a degree from Yale. Then it was my turn. I proudly announced that I had gone to Notre Dame. I might as well have said that I graduated from Sing Sing. Instead of nodding and smiling, as they had for the other universities, the bankers in that oak-paneled dining room cleared their throats and politely looked away. Notre Dame was a respectable enough school if you were a football player—or a Catholic. Otherwise, it wasn't on the map.

Today, being a WASP is not as important as it used to be, and neither is attending an Ivy League school. True, a lot of people still believe deep in their hearts that graduates of private schools are somehow better people. But thanks to business leaders like Bill Gates (a Harvard drop-out), the rule that you had to graduate from an Ivy League school is beginning to change. So is the more disturbing rule that you had to be white, male, and heterosexual. Although the changes are slower than they ought to be, the business world is starting to look like America—which is not to imply that all barriers to success have been removed. Cliques still exist. The old boy network still exists. Racism, sexism, and religious intolerance have not disappeared and neither has ageism. But they're fading fast—not because of federal laws (although I certainly think Lyndon Johnson's Civil Rights legislation was helpful), but because talented and open-minded people are demonstrating different ways of doing things.

Conform or Else

I wonder whether anyone born after, say, 1967, can have any idea of what a stranglehold convention once had on this country. In the 1940s and 1950s, if you didn't conform, you were the odd man out—and that was not a good thing. Men wore suits and ties: that rule was so firmly entrenched that when the Beatles appeared on the *Ed Sullivan Show* in 1964, even *they* wore suits and ties. Women standing behind the counters at Saks literally wore white gloves. With very few exceptions, work was nine to five. Original ideas were distrusted, and so were flamboyant, outspoken people. John F. Kennedy was a breath of fresh air for many reasons, not the least of which was, unlike Dwight D. Eisenhower, he had a personality.

But if conformity stifled creativity and individuality, it also offered something we lack today: security. If you toed the line at work, you had a job for life. The corporation would take care of you from your first paycheck to your gold watch and beyond.

Today, people want a freer life. They want to enjoy themselves more, and they don't want to feel limited or pinned down. This is true not just in the United States but all over the world. Even the Organization Man doesn't want to be the organization man anymore.

The Lost Virtues

Although bigotry and conformity were commonplace when I began my business career, not every aspect of that long-ago time was negative. For instance, loyalty was assumed. It no longer is. Today people change jobs, voluntarily and otherwise, at a dizzying rate.

A recent article in *Business 2.0* described several employees who left established firms (like Hewlett-Packard) to sign on with start-ups. When the dot.com deluge struck, they ran screaming back to the mother ship. And guess what? The corporations welcomed them back.

When I started out in business, neither part of that story could have happened. Employees were not cavalier about leaving good jobs at solid companies, and corporations weren't so ready to take them back. Although this job-hopping frenzy may have peaked, thanks to growing unemployment and a widespread anxiety about the future, no one can doubt that the rules have changed. In a sense, everyone has become a free agent. Job-switching is not only not frowned upon, it's expected. So if you're a corporate manager, you can't count on your staff to stay with you. (Tip: Treating them very, very well helps.) And if you're an employee, it doesn't matter how high you are on the totem pole: your job is vulnerable. In 2000, forty of the 200 largest companies in the United States let their chief executives go. No one is bullet-proof. Just ask Ted Turner.

Civility is another lost virtue. It used to be the rule, not the exception. Today, people say virtually anything they want to. They're insulting, rude, and vulgar. (Of course, maybe every generation, once it's no longer caught up in the rebelliousness of youth, comes to believe that things used to be more civilized. I think of "Anything Goes," Cole Porter's great song bemoaning the loss of civility. It was written in 1934.)

Nonetheless, it seems to me that today, a lack of civility taints the most ordinary encounters. For instance, when I first came to work in New York City, I used to go to a sidewalk stand in the morning to get breakfast. We would all stand in line in an ordered way, buy a bagel and coffee, and carry it upstairs to the office. Today, there are thirty people milling around at the stand, there is no line, and everybody's yelling as they push forward. Chaos has replaced civility.

Even in the rarefied world of big business, civility has taken a hit. I'm reminded of a meeting I arranged between two high-powered executives. I thought they might be able to do business together. But right before the meeting, one of the men, the CEO of a large company, confided that he intended to insult the other guy in order to get his attention.

I said, you don't have to do that. The proposition you're offering is powerful enough to carry the day on its own. You ought to do this in a low key, understated way. Then wait for his reaction.

The CEO was adamant. He was determined to do it his way. And he did. The other guy was so offended that he literally walked out of the room. It took over two weeks—two wasted weeks—to get them back together. Personally, I favor a more civilized approach.

Finally, the atmosphere of the business world has been damaged in one other way. Thanks in part to a hyperactive plaintiff bar, it has been infected by a barrage of lawsuits on everything from age and minority discrimination to sexual harassment. Many of these suits are legitimate. But many are frivolous, caused not only by disgruntled employees but by big-mouth bosses who ought to know that sometimes it's wise to be guarded about what you say.

What Happened?

Pinpointing reasons why the world has changed is never easy. But I'd like to give it a whirl. I think there are three basic causes:

The changing role of government

I spend a lot of time in Washington, D.C., and I am not happy about what goes on there. It seems to me that government is failing and our basic systems are in need of repair. For instance, I don't think anybody is satisfied with our educational system in the United States. Half our kids can't read, particularly in large urban areas. The schools themselves are in disrepair. And there's a dearth of qualified teachers. Well, no wonder. There's something wrong with a system in which a Dallas Cowboys quarterback makes ninety million dollars while a high school teacher struggles for less than forty thousand a year.

Medical care is another problem. Was Hillary Clinton's health care plan on the right track? I don't know. But it was certainly a bungled opportunity. A partial plan would have been better than nothing.

And then there's the legal profession. There are approximately

50,000 lawyers in Washington, D.C., alone—five times as many as in 1970. Many of them are lawmakers who are pork-barreling like mad instead of dealing with the common good. As a result, business and government, which used to be largely separate, are joined at the hip and the number of lobbyists both in Washington and in Brussels, the headquarters of the European Union, has increased dramatically. A lot of the companies I deal with, knowing that the ability to access government is crucial to their success, have developed carefully thought-out strategies for governmental relations. Lobbying to get laws passed is an integral part of what they do. Twenty-five years ago, that simply wasn't the case.

Greed

I don't want to sound like a preacher, but the climate has changed and I think that old-fashioned greed has a lot to do with it. It's our Sodom and Gomorrah. We have become profligate and so successful as a country that we have lost our sense of balance. People expect to achieve a level of financial independence that was once inconceivable for anyone other than royalty and robber barons. I suppose they imagine that ever-increasing wealth will lead to ever-increasing happiness. If only it could.

Technology

When I started working in the 1960s, the IBM Selectric typewriter represented a major technological advance, carbon paper was still being perfected, and the usual way to send an important message was to mail it, which took two or three days at best. If you were corresponding with someone in another country, it could take as long as a week. If you were communicating with people in a remote location, you could never be sure if your message arrived at all. I remember having to dispatch messengers to parts of Central Asia, South America, and Africa just because we weren't sure the mail would get through. With today's technology, the concept of "remote" is becoming extinct—and you know in a heartbeat whether you got through. Just as the internal combustion engine transformed society by making it possible to travel quickly between distant spots, the computer has thoroughly altered our world. Today, all bets are off. The old assumptions are no longer valid. The rules have changed.

Twenty-First Century Rules

Doing business today is more demanding than ever, and more daunting. It requires intelligence, energy, resilience, global awareness, and old-fashioned street smarts. Here are the rules:

1. Add value. A company recently asked me to promote their CEO. When I asked what distinguished him, I was told that he used to be a referee in the National Football League and had relationships with a lot of football players. Anyone who knows me will tell you that I'm a sports nut. Nonetheless, I wasn't impressed, because this company had absolutely nothing to do with sports. The CEO's football experience was irrelevant to the business. It did not add value.

To add value, you need to have fresh ideas, startling insights, knowledge, skill, or economic savvy. One way or another, unless you bring something to the table, you may find that your seat has been taken.

In my office, the basic rule is this: If you come to the meeting you had better have something to say—and if you don't have something to say, don't come to the meeting. This simple rule makes a huge difference.

For example, a few months ago, a group of us attended an important meeting in Toronto. I reminded everyone in advance that they should be prepared to add value. The week before the meeting, each one of them went out and did research. When we came together, that additional data coalesced and raised our level of participation far beyond what it could have been. In the meeting, we offered our client new ways to think about his business, new ways to price his product, trends that were coming from competitors, and all kinds of other information. This wasn't just another routine meeting where we offered a bit of advice to a client. This was an extraordinary experience. Afterwards, the client wrote me a letter and said that he'd never attended such a meeting before. It was a success because everyone in that room, working individually, had figured out a way to add value.

Adding value in this way requires an open mind and a fearless disposition. One executive I know who has those qualities in spades works for a major food company in the Middle West. When this guy is facing a difficult problem, he takes the Jack Kennedy approach. He seeks out the best and the brightest to work on it. He brings in legal minds, financial minds, public relations minds— the best in the world. The meeting is designed as a wide-ranging and open discussion with one rule: Park your ego at the door. As a result of that, I've seen him come up with one original solution after another. He's not afraid to add value.

2. Be inclusive. No one is suggesting that you have to hire every Tom, Dick, and Harriet. You don't have to include people who don't measure up. But you can't exclude people in the ways that they have been excluded in the past. If you're not inclusive both in your hiring practices and in the way you conceive of your market, you're going to be counted out.

Besides that, being inclusive is good for business. Big advertisers like Pepsi Cola, Procter & Gamble, and the Ford Motor Company understand the importance of inclusion because they recognize how critical it is to deal with the Hispanic market, the African-American market, and other similar markets. They know if they understand those markets, they can tap into them, which will help their bottom line. Being inclusive offers a significant competitive advantage.

More important, it's the right thing to do.

Although The Dilenschneider Group, I'm glad to report, is a rainbow company, I admit that I was put to the test when I interviewed Scott Chesney. I knew that he'd been an accomplished athlete, but I didn't know that a rare medical disorder had unexpectedly confined him to a wheelchair for the rest of his life. So when he wheeled himself into my office, I was stunned. Throughout the interview, I kept thinking, How can I employ this guy?

I decided to give it a shot. We made Chesney a researcher. He worked on the computer and was very helpful to the company. Our objective was to have him present research reports. So we brought him into meetings. We took him on trips. And he made a significant contribution.

Then one day he announced that he was going to take a round-the-world cruise and create a business. To no one's surprise, it's quite successful. Being in a wheelchair hasn't held him back.

One of the most inclusive people I know is Marilyn Carlson Nelson, the CEO of Carlson Companies, Inc. Her business, which owns cruise ships, TGIFridays, Radisson Hotels, and more, is bigger than American Express, with an extraordinary footprint all over the world. It employs thousands of people—and I wouldn't be surprised if Marilyn's met them all. Oftentimes when Marilyn is working on a problem, she draws a circle around it, and she always draws that circle big enough to include everybody. She will go out of her way to talk with the desk clerk. She makes a point of being inclusive—and her attitude is not faked. Does it work? Marilyn is probably the number one female business executive in the world. But then I've noticed that the more successful people are, the more inclusive they tend to be.

At the same time, it's disturbing that the old shibboleths, resentments, and intolerances still exist, especially among older people.

Racism still exists, there's no question about it. To this day, I think that African Americans face incredible hurdles in getting major jobs in big business (which is not to say that it doesn't happen, as the ascension of Richard Parsons to the chief executive spot at AOL Time Warner clearly indicates).

Similarly, anti-Semitism is a problem. We can pretend that it has been licked but it has not been licked. I see it all over the place.

And I have to say that many older men have an anti-female bias that is unimaginable. In part, this happens because their attitudes have been locked in for years, and in part because females are becoming so successful in the workplace that men are running scared. I work with a man who essentially refuses to work with women. I can put females next to him, and he will tolerate them because he knows if he doesn't, I'll talk to him harshly. But he never gives them an even break. The fact is that if he gave these women a chance, his job would be easier and his output would be better. But he doesn't do it.

Is he making a big mistake? You bet he is. Today, if you're not open and inclusive, you've got a serious problem. Sooner or later, you can expect it to backfire.

3. Think globally and culturally. When I was growing up, everyone said that the United States was a melting pot. Frankly, I didn't see it. Today, I work in New York City, where according to the 2000 census, 40 percent of the population is foreign-born, and I see it every day. The guy who owns the grocery store is Korean; the lab technician comes from India; the taxi driver is from Haiti by way of Canada; the intern in my office is from Jordan. And I could go on. We're in a global environment that is unprecedented. No matter what business you're in, you're not going to be dealing with a bunch of Presbyterians and Rotarians any longer. Your colleagues and your customers hail from all walks of life and all parts of the globe, and you've got to be able to think in their terms. If you don't, you're going to get shut out.

Yet by and large, Americans are quite parochial. Only 17 percent of us have passports, compared to something like 80 percent of the British. I'm shocked by that statistic. Being closed off to the rest of the world is not only a cultural loss, it's a business disaster.

By thinking globally, you can create unparalleled opportunities. For instance, I know a man named John Bonsignori who ran a small mail order business selling electronic parts for audio and video systems. One day he got on the web where, if you know what you're doing, you can really expand your business. John found linkages for his business throughout Central Asia. Communicating via fax and e-mail, he identified totally new markets. He became very successful and reasonably wealthy because he was able to think globally.

At the same time, it's imperative to understand that the global environment operates differently from the local environment. There are people around the world whose experiences are vastly less privileged than ours. And business practices are far from universal—as anyone knows who's done business in Japan, Russia, or Eastern Europe. They approach business very differently from the way we do. If you're not smart enough to recognize their cultural patterns and think in their terms, you're going to make mistakes.

For instance, if I'm talking to the Belgians, I know that they want to walk around the problem again and again and again before they come to a conclusion—and I've got to let them do it. If I'm talking to the Chinese, I know it's a negotiation, no matter what happens. If I'm doing business in India, I know that before we get down to the issue at hand, there's a period of rhetoric that oftentimes has virtually nothing to do with the problem. These are cultural patterns, and you need to be aware of them.

It's also important to remember that in addition to our freedom and our military might, we enjoy a standard of living in this country that exists virtually nowhere else on earth. So, yes, people resent us. That means if I act like an aggressive New Yorker or a brash American, I will lose every time. Coca-Cola found this out in Brussels. Jack Welch, the legendary CEO of General Electric, found this out in his failed attempt to acquire Honeywell International. I think we're going to see more cross-border deals in the future. Unless you understand the cultural environment you're in, you're going to shut the door on significant opportunities.

4. Think strategically, not just tactically. Thinking strategically means having a goal, understanding the long-range implications of your actions, and acting accordingly.

To do that, you need to know what your objectives are. Yet many of us stumble along from day to day without defining our goals. Recently, I sat down to list mine. I was thinking about Lou Holtz, the famous football coach. Around 1967, he created a master list of 107 things he hoped to accomplish in his life. Those goals covered everything from family and finances to his desire to be invited to dinner at the White House. Since then, he has accomplished ninety-five of those goals—and counting. "It's not a wish list," he said. "It's a set of things I wanted to accomplish and it really hasn't changed that much."

I decided to emulate him (although, in recognition of my advanced age, I cut the list in half). I wrote down fifty things and I prioritized them. In addition to professional and financial goals, my list included the following: I'd like to attend an entire World

Series. I want to understand the architecture behind the great cathedral at Chartres. I'd like to sail up the coast of Alaska. And so forth.

Once you've got a list, you can develop a five year (or ten year) plan. Without one, you're sailing without a compass. There is no better way to keep yourself on course.

I recently agreed to work with a man who's the head of a big French company. I'm excited about working with him. But I don't want to focus on his concerns so narrowly that I limit myself. Instead, I'm hoping that the work I do for him will encourage him to lead me to other French companies. For that to happen, I need to keep the big picture in mind. And I need to think strategically.

Here's another example, one that I hope you won't have to emulate. It concerns my good friend, Harry (not his real name, for reasons you will understand). Harry is facing a serious law suit concerning a troublesome series of events that happened in the 1970s. His lawyers have proven beyond a shadow of a doubt that Harry did nothing wrong in that situation. He is sure to be exonerated. However, in the course of proving his innocence in the 1970s, his lawyers unearthed something heinous that he did in the 1980s. Harry is worried now that the other side will find out about this. He also wants to make sure that his supporters—who keep encouraging him to proclaim his innocence—don't find out about his 1980s problem. So he's got to think strategically about how to approach one case without opening up the other. He needs a long-term strategy.

People always think tactically. And the more ambitious people are, the more tactically driven they are. They want to win every battle. That can be shortsighted. What matters most is being able to look several moves ahead like a skilled chess player who can see well in advance what the repercussions of losing a pawn or taking a knight might be.

Richard Nixon called it linkage. Whether you like him or not, he deserves credit for pioneering that kind of thinking in the public arena. Linkage means that you don't do things episodically any longer. You think about the way things are connected, and you approach them strategically.

But you can only do that effectively if you have some sense of where you're heading.

5. Be technologically able. I used to think that I didn't need technology. My brains will get me there, I thought. I was so wrong.

People who are resistant to the computer—and most of those people are north of fifty—are making a gigantic mistake. If you're not up to speed technologically, you don't stand a chance. At minimum, that means being acquainted with a computer, a fax, a cell phone, and a PDA. It means keeping up with software, understanding the language of computers, being able to navigate your way around the Internet without begging a teenager for help, and being prepared for the day when you too will carry around a tiny, hand-held device that enables you to send e-mail while you're in line at the movies. Is it easy? Frankly, no. It's a constant battle. And Bill Gates and his colleagues are making it worse because they're inventing more stuff all the time.

Of course, there are times when it's smarter to opt for an old-fashioned methodology—like using the public library rather than, say, Google. I don't mean to denigrate the Internet. It's endlessly fascinating. But if you rely on it alone, you are limited. While there's a wealth of material available in cyberspace, not everything is on the computer—and a lot of what is available is junk. Don't throw away your library card.

And don't forget about the post office, either. Personal letters have become such a rarity that people are thrilled to get one, especially if it's handwritten. In many ways, snail mail can actually be more effective than faxes or e-mail or video conferences.

One person who understands that is Elizabeth Dole, former head of the American Red Cross. I served on its board with her for twelve years and I saw how effectively she used the handwritten note. She wrote them herself and there was always a personal element to them. I received many of these notes. Could she have e-mailed me? Yes, and did. But those e-mails weren't as effective—or as memorable—as the handwritten notes.

The real question to ask yourself is this: What's the most effective way to get through? E-mail is often the best way, especially when speed is of the essence. But as someone who receives up to

200 e-mail messages a day, I can tell you that e-mail has a down-side. Many people delete certain messages sight unseen, or their e-mail is read by assistants who make their own judgments about what's important. Your message may never get through. Writing a note or letter can have a greater impact than sending e-mail—especially if you have a facility with language and an understanding of how to put something down on paper. That's an advantage that younger people don't necessarily enjoy.

Finally, you can increase your advantage still more by hiring a messenger service and having the letter hand-delivered. I guarantee you, that letter will be read.

6. Deal in substance rather than technique. Style is not enough. Technique is not enough. You need substantive ideas, real-life examples, and hard facts. I can come up with a great envelope but if there's nothing to put in it, I don't have much (though Harvey Mackay, envelope entrepreneur and author of *Swim With the Sharks Without Being Eaten Alive,* might disagree).

In my line of work, it is common to focus on technique. For many of my colleagues, that's where the fun is. They love to ask questions like: how can we make this maneuver, how do we negotiate this contact, how should we arrange this meeting, what color do we use, how do we dress this thing up? They love to spin—a concept I deplore.

Substance is so much more important than that. I used to work with a man named Roy Battersby. Clients would say Roy, we want this news release in the paper, and Roy would look at it and say, I can't get it in the paper for you. There's nothing there. He'd turn them down flat.

One time, I said, but Roy, shouldn't we at least try to get this news release in the paper?

Look, he told me. If the client has something of substance, they can send it to the newspaper scrawled on butcher paper with a crayon, and the paper will use it. If there's nothing substantive, nothing I can do will convince them to use it.

I've never forgotten that lesson in substance. Although all fields suffer from the problem to some extent, public relations is particularly susceptible to the lure of technique. Let's face it: A lot of PR people live in the world of smoke and mirrors. You never

quite understand exactly what they have to say because they're trying to put one over on you. It's a mistake. Stick to the substance.

I learned that one December in the 1970s, when I introduced
a product called Gatorade during a playoff game between the Los
Angeles Rams and the Minnesota Vikings. Before the game began,
we served steaming hot Gatorade to the Rams and cold Gatorade
to the Vikings. The idea was, Gatorade gets into your system fast,
and drinking it hot will make your hands more supple. At half-
time, the Rams were ahead. They came over and said, hey, this hot
Gatorade is working, and they clapped me on the back and told
me I was a great human.

But in the final minutes of the game, Guy Henderson caught a
pass and the Vikings won. My reputation as a human took a plunge.

Yet the truth is, Gatorade really does have something going for
it. It's approved by the FDA because it has an isotonic quality,
which means that it gets into your bloodstream faster than water
and replenishes the liquid in your system whether you drink it
hot, cold, or at room temperature.

I'm a Rams fan. I wanted them to win that game. But I have to
admit: If they had won, we might all be sipping hot Gatorade
today.

7. Be a stand-up person. In the past, if something wasn't on the
up-and-up, everybody kept quiet. The blue wall of silence, as the
police call it, was equally operative in the business community.
People were reluctant to step forward. Today, the climate has
changed.

Dick Fuld, the CEO of Lehman Brothers, is an example. Time
after time, he stood up for brokers and traders who were fifty-five
or sixty years old and who were in danger of being dismissed because their advanced age made younger people uncomfortable.
Dick has literally stood in the doorway to prevent experienced
people from being fired. I think that attitude is one of the reasons
for Lehman Brothers' incredible success.

There are times when it's easy to avoid being a stand-up person. I once had a client who for unknown reasons shut me out.
Suddenly, I no longer had access. She kept me on retainer, but it
was clear that I was out in the cold.

Was I upset? A little. Was I tempted to take my ball and go

home? I was. But I wanted to act like a professional, so I continued to keep an eye on her company. Months later, I realized that she badly needed my advice. I swallowed my pride and called her up to offer it. Working together, we solved the problem. She overcame her embarrassment. I overcame my injured feelings. Plus, I felt good because I knew I had done the right thing.

The chief advantage of being a stand-up person is this: At the end of the day, you can live with yourself.

8. Be creative. Thirty or forty years ago, creativity was a concept that applied solely to the arts. That's no longer the case—and I say, thank you, Bill Gates. Along with many other people, he's opened up a plethora of opportunities that have led to, among other things, an explosion of small, home-grown businesses and more scientific breakthroughs than ever before. The amount of data that you can access today, and the ways you can knit that data together, lend themselves to a level of creative expression that has never before been possible.

9. Be a maverick. You might think that in the world of business, being a maverick would be a liability. But it ain't necessarily so. Look at Herb Kelleher, the founder of Southwest Airlines. Or Ted Turner. Or Jane Fonda, for that matter. These people have always insisted on going their own way. And they have been extraordinarily successful.

The truth is, it helps to stand out from the crowd. And the older you are, the easier and more natural it is. When young people try to stand out, there's often a forced quality to their efforts. People in their fifties and sixties have the confidence to distinguish themselves without dying their hair green. They do it by expressing their opinions.

Even on a small scale, I've seen how effective this is. For instance, my wife and I enjoy giving dinner parties. I've noticed that the people who express themselves most vividly take a risk, especially if they voice contrary or unusual opinions. But afterwards, the other guests remember who they are. The good gray guest, who politely sits at the table and is agreeable, makes no impact. Don't do that to yourself. Speak up. Some people will disagree with you. But so what? Not only will you have a better time, you'll make a greater impression. And the likelihood is that by expressing your opinions, you'll be more effective. As Thomas Jefferson said to John Adams, "Opinion is power."

10. Be street smart. Twenty years ago, members of the business community felt sheltered by the corporations, by convention, by a host of factors. The sense of security may have been an illusion. But we felt it all the same.

Today, you've got to be street smart—and it doesn't matter what street you're on. Even on Park Avenue, where my office is located, you've got to watch your back. You've got to be wise to human nature.

That means understanding that what people say is not always what they mean; that self-interest is a powerful motivator; that actions speak louder than words; that it's a competitive world out there. You had better be prepared.

Being street smart means understanding that power arises in many forms. Some people use avoidance as a power tool. Other people use intimidation. Position brings power. So does money, and not just because you can buy things with it. For instance, there are many private clubs. Those clubs appear to be social, but a lot of business goes on in those hushed, high-ceilinged rooms. If your bank account isn't up to snuff, you'll never get in. Money conveys the power to keep people out.

You might argue that power is part of the human condition, as Machiavelli pointed out. But thirty or forty years ago, power belonged only to those who understood it intuitively, wanted it desperately, or had it thrust upon them. Today, there are many power-hungry people, especially in business, who have studied it avidly, who know how to use it, and who calculate their moves with the concentration that, say, Serena Williams brings to a game of tennis. These people are your competitors. So if you don't know how to serve and volley on the courts of power, you're at a severe disadvantage.

What should you do if you feel like a lamb among lions? These are the rules of the street:

- Be honest at all times. You don't always have to be forthcoming. Omission is not usually a crime. But if you're engaged with somebody and you're dishonest, you will inevitably be caught.

- Know your own motives. Try to understand those of other people. And—I hate to say it—be suspicious. Very few people do things solely for altruistic reasons, no matter what they say.
- Be respectful to other people at all times. If you're not, the street will rise up and bite you.
- Control your anger. Throwing a tantrum is obviously foolish but letting your anger leak out slowly is also a mistake.
- Be aware. Watch your back. And protect yourself—physically, emotionally, and mentally.

I knew a man named Nick Inglesia who used to work for Revlon. He told me something I've never forgotten: There are people who make things happen, there are people who watch things happen, and there are people who wonder what happened.

The only way to make sure you're never in the third category is to remember: It's a rough world out there, and the rules have changed. Ignore them at your peril.

2

The Lay of the Land

I was born in the midst of World War II so I am not a member of the Baby Boom generation (though I would argue that anyone who enjoys the music of the 1960s as much as I do ought to be accorded honorary status).

Nonetheless, like everyone else of working age, whether they were born before 1946, when the Baby Boom began, or after 1964, when it officially came to an end, I have been affected by it. The Baby Boom represents such a huge bulge in the population that it has been described as a pig moving through a python. Its power to shape the culture, influence public policy, and affect the economy is immense. Other demographic groups—including Generation-X, which understandably worries about having to support the boomers in their dotage—complain that boomer concerns receive excessive attention. They may be right. But that doesn't change the situation—because, like it or not, the Baby is calling the shots.

Look at the figures. As of 2000, there were approximately 82 million Baby Boomers in the United States. (That includes immigrants, who make up approximately 10 percent of the total.) At every step along the way, their concerns have dominated society.

In 1946, when the boom began, *Dr. Spock's Baby and Child Care* was published. It ultimately sold more copies than the Bible. A few years later, as a friend of mine remarked, "they created the suburbs for us." Levittown, the ultimate symbol of the 1950s, offered its first pre-assembled Cape Cod two-bedroom in 1947, its first ranch house in 1949. Ten years later, Mattel introduced Barbie, the prototypical teenage doll and the most successful toy ever made (one billion sold). The oldest Baby Boomers had just entered their teens. Coincidence? I think not.

When the Baby Boomers were ready for college, the educational system had to accommodate them. The result? Open admissions, the expansion of the community college system, and, in the 1970s, the creation of 743 new colleges.

As they aged, Baby Boomers carried the population with them. No sooner did the Baby Boom end in 1964 than the median age began to creep upwards. In the early 1970s, the median age was 28. In 1990, it was 32.9. Today, it's over 35. The Baby Boom, which once vowed never to trust anyone over thirty, has presided over the graying of America.

That trend will continue. Between 1995 and 2005, the number of Americans aged fifty to sixty-four is expected to increase by over 40 percent. Between now and 2025, the over-fifty-five population will increase more dramatically than any other age group.

The influence that segment of the population wields is likely to grow as well. That doesn't mean that age discrimination is not a problem. If you work in Hollywood and you're over fifty—or forty, or maybe even thirty—you're in deep trouble. The picture is also grim in the advertising industry, which has been the target of about 20 percent of all age discrimination suits. Studies clearly indicate that once you hit forty—not fifty—getting a job in the business world becomes measurably more difficult. Not surprisingly, experts predict the number of age discrimination suits to rise.

Nonetheless, Baby Boomers have made it clear that they expect to keep working, even beyond retirement. Whether they decide to work part-time, become consultants, open their own businesses, or freelance, they will not be side-lined.

But to do that successfully, it's essential to be aware of the environment we're in. After a decade of prosperity, that environment is uncertain at best.

It's the Economy, Stupid

These are uncertain economic times for four fundamental reasons:

- Technology has changed the world utterly. Although we have had the opportunity to explore technology in this country, it's only beginning to spread around the world. Soon the rest of the world will have the advantages of technology. They'll be able to put their imaginations to work, which means that things will become more competitive. How will that affect us? We have no idea.
- Outside the United States, there is a lamentable lack of transparency or reliable, publicly available business and economic data. In the United States, we have many forms of regulation including the SEC, the New York Stock Exchange, and the IRS. As a result, information is readily available. Around the world, things are considerably more veiled. This lack of transparency is going to create a serious problem.
- In a global world, the economy of one country can significantly upset the economy of another without most people realizing what's happening. For example, if the Japanese decided to cash in their United States treasuries, it would create a massive problem in the United States. If the oil-rich countries of the Persian Gulf decide to put the clamps on production, that would create a problem. There are huge socio-economic-political problems occurring around the world, and they are making life uncertain.
- The terrorist attacks of September 11 have altered everyone's priorities, economically and otherwise. The long-term implications of this are completely unknown.

In many ways, we find ourselves in a brave new economy. We don't know what to expect. Despite rising unemployment, we have assets and fundamentals in place that, at least in the short run, will ensure the future of the United States. But the global environment is going to change radically over the next fifteen or twenty years. Today's models and paradigms are bound to mutate, and the climate will change. Predicting the future will be harder than ever. Sure, people will speculate on it, and some of them will be right. They'll be able to look back in twenty years and say, I nailed it.

The rest of us can only hope not to get nailed ourselves.

The Uncertainty Principle

Investing in an uncertain economy is always a challenge, but if you're over fifty, it's a challenge with a bite because you can't afford to be wrong. What to do? These are the basics:

1. Consider the economy you're in and act accordingly. If you happen to be reading this at a time when everything looks golden, you're in luck. An up economy is the best time to plan your financial future—but only if you account for the very real possibility of economic downturns. That way, when the inevitable occurs, you'll be prepared.

If the economy is in trouble, don't let your anxieties paralyze you, because investment opportunities proliferate during economic slowdowns. The ideal time to invest is when the market has hit bottom. True, it's not easy to know when that has happened. And it's not easy to act on that understanding. Buying a stock when it has seemingly tanked is counterintuitive at best. But it's the smart thing to do. As Mark Twain said, "Buy low, sell high." That may be self-evident, but it's still a worthy goal.

2. Understand that we have moved from an economy of investing to an economy of trading. Conventional wisdom used to be that the smart thing to do was to invest for the long term and watch your money slowly accumulate. If you're over fifty and you're not financially set, you may not have that luxury. You've got to be an intelligent trader. So what do you do? Read *Barron's* every week—cover to cover. Read *IDD, Investment Dealers' Digest*. It's a trade magazine that most people don't know about, and it's packed with advice worth considering. Read *Pensions and Investments*. Read some of the arcane publications that most people ignore because the writers in those publications are on top of what's

going on and generally give pretty good advice. Or read people like Lawrence Kudlow or Charles Kadlec (more about him in a minute), men who understand the economy in a deep way.

What shouldn't you do? First: Don't pay attention to most television gurus. Many of them don't have a clue about what's going on.

Second: Ignore the tens of thousands of so-called investment advisors who don't know much more than you do about the market but feel confident enough to hang out a shingle and give advice, often based on little more than curbstone suggestions.

Keep in mind, even the experts have a tough time, as *USA Today* revealed in a fascinating experiment. In January, 2001, *USA Today* asked ten highly touted Wall Street strategists to recommend a few stocks. Seven months later, the Dow declined 5 percent, Standard & Poor's 500 dropped 10 percent, and the Nasdaq fell 19 percent. How did the so-called experts do? Not so well. The stocks they chose were down by a full 22 percent. In a rocky market, financial advice can be a game of chance. Recently, even untouchable investment advisors such as Henry Blodget (dubbed "King Henry" by the *Wall Street Journal*) and Mary "Queen of the Net" Meeker, the highest paid woman on Wall Street (her base salary was $15 million), have come under the gun for their mistakes. So you've got to be cautious. You can't leave your investments entirely in someone else's hands.

On the other hand, I don't mean to suggest that you should go it alone. On the contrary; you'd be foolish not to engage the services of a professional. But go in with your eyes open. You've got to be knowledgeable enough to participate in the conversation. (If you need a recommendation, take a look at Worth.com, the website of *Worth Magazine*, which publishes a state-by-state list of the top 250 financial advisers in the nation.)

3. Figure out what you need—and think about downsizing. I look at it this way: Nobody has gotten out of life alive. We all die sooner or later. And if you think about the statistical tables and you look at the genes in your family, you can figure out, roughly, how many years you have left.

I admit, this exercise is not for the faint of heart. But if you force yourself to do it, it can be incredibly useful. Figure out how much money you need per year and multiply that by the number of years you figure you have left (and be generous, just in case you surprise yourself and live for a long time, as the Baby Boomers are expected to do). Then do the calculations, not forgetting to factor in your pension, your social security, and any money you stand to inherit. Are you on track? Do you need to earn more? Should you cut back your expenses now in hopes of accumulating more for later? Even a small reduction can make a big difference.

For instance, if you like to travel and you're worried about money, you'd be a fool not to surf the web. To buy an airline ticket over the counter today is absolutely crazy.

You also have to think about how you want to live and what you want to have. Do you own a big house? Then you know how much effort it takes to keep it up. Do you really want to spend your time calling people to clean the furnace or check the lawn sprinklers? At a certain point, I think the answer is no. Time is the most precious commodity you have. You should spend it doing things you want to do.

4. In an uncertain economy, it's wise to look at commodities that don't generally decrease in value. I'm talking about real estate, precious metals, art, and antiques. In a down economy, these areas can offer extraordinary bargains.

5. Be conservative in your investments. If you look at the companies that were part of the so-called nifty fifty around 1970, very few of them are around today. Blue chips, once the sine qua non of wise investing, are not necessarily the way to go. The companies leading the market today have names that didn't exist ten years ago, and ten years from now people will be making big bucks on companies that do not exist today. Given that, what does it mean to invest conservatively? It does not mean sinking every cent you've got into bonds, though a down market generally inspires people to look in that direction. I'd say the hallmark of conservative investing is, as always, to diversify.

Bulls and Bears

After many years of a bull market, it can be distressing when the bears appear, as they did in 2000. Despite rising unemployment, high debt levels, and falling revenues, not everyone predicted disaster.

Writing in 1999, investment strategist Harry S. Dent, Jr., author of *The Roaring 2000s Investor,* was convinced that the boom of the 1990s would continue because the Baby Boomers would continue to fuel the market. As a result, he suggested, boom times would continue—with the occasional correction. The economy, he suggested, would be especially robust between the end of 2002 and 2008 or 2009. At the end of those seven fat years, he estimated that the Dow could be at thirty-five or forty thousand. But at that point, the Baby Boomers would start to retire—and that, according to Dent, is when the market will start to go south. He foresaw a deflationary downturn that would last around thirteen years, from 2009 to 2022 or 2023, when the Dow might be as low as ten or fifteen thousand.

Needless to say, not everyone accepts this scenario. Take economist Charles Kadlec of J. & W. Seligman & Co., Inc. He definitely doesn't expect the stock market to crash in ten years. In *Dow 100,000: Fact or Fiction,* he explores the possibility that by 2020, the Dow could be in the six figures. Here's part of my conversation with him:

CHARLES KADLEC

RD: *You wrote* Dow 100,000: Fact or Fiction *in 1999. Are you as optimistic now as you were then?*

CK: I'm more optimistic, actually. The pieces are in place to create a Great Prosperity, one of the consequences of which could be the Dow reaching 100,000 by the year 2020. It looks like an extraordinary number because we don't think in geometric or log scales. It's a ten-fold increase from here, which is what we experienced between 1981, when the Dow was at a thousand, and 1999, when the Dow hit ten thousand. So we've already lived through an equivalent tenfold increase in the Dow.

RD: *What factors do you think stimulated the Great Prosperity?*

CK: The single biggest factor is the end of the Cold War because it changed the social and political dynamic of our time. It's important to recognize that the Cold War was a real war. With the exception of Korea and Vietnam, not a lot of people got killed. But they had nuclear missiles aimed at us and we had nuclear weapons aimed at them, and both sides were spending a lot of money on weapons and resources to fight the war.

Then the Cold War ended. When wars end, societies typically reduce tax rates, restore monetary stability, and allow freer trade. All over the world, societies with governments both left of center and right of center are doing those three things. And what our research at Seligman shows is that during periods of falling tax rates, monetary stability, and freer trade, you get above average growth and above average equity returns.

But the Great Prosperity is far from a sure thing. We'll make mistakes along the way. The key question is, will the mistakes be self-correcting or will they be the kind of mistakes that ultimately end prosperities? We've seen a series of mistakes in the last couple of years. In the year 2000, for example, we had a bad monetary policy. The Fed was way too tight, way too long. The tax burden was rising as people's incomes were rising and they were getting pushed into higher tax brackets. And we had an oil shock. In 2001, tax rate reductions were mostly deferred in favor of tax rebates and other gimmicks. The Fed fell into a deflationary monetary policy. However, the overall response has been positive. We've begun to get better monetary policy, although we're not out of the woods yet. We've gotten some tax rate relief, modest in the short term but building over time. And the oil shock is self-correcting. These are very different responses than what happened in Japan. When its stock market fell sharply and its economy slowed, they raised taxes, persisted in a deflationary monetary policy, and pulled back from free trade. Ten years later, they're still pursuing those same failed policies. I'm actually encouraged by the policy response in the United States.

RD: *So these recent economic downturns don't disturb you?*

CK: No. The economy is a dynamic system and errors are inevitable. That's why we have corrections in the stock market. They bring forth corrective actions, and as long as that happens, the direction of the economy will be positive. That's not saying that there won't be rolling recessions. But as long as the basic impulse toward lower tax rates, price stability, and freer trade is driving the system, the historical record is clear. During these periods, on average, people are very good at finding a way to make a better and more prosperous world.

RD: *Are you worried about the demise of the dot.coms?*

CK: No. Companies that aren't turning profits inevitably go out of business. So what? The wonderful thing about capitalism is that you can't squander resources forever. If you can't generate positive cash flow, the system shuts you down. Look at the history of the automobile. Over a hundred car companies went out of business. A few great companies survived and changed the world.

Something similar is happening now. In the short term these companies are going through a classical boom-bust. But the technological revolution is in the earliest stage, and it's fueling the Great Prosperity. The internet is breaking down the barriers of time and distance to trade. It's the biggest commercial thoroughfare ever invented, and despite the glitches, it's creating a period of accelerating trade. That will lead to greater prosperity.

RD: *Is there anything out there that could jeopardize the Great Prosperity?*

CK: From my perspective, there are three significant threats to the world economy and to my optimistic viewpoint. The first is the first war of the twenty-first century, the war on terrorism. Wars are bad for an economy. The attacks on the World Trade Center and the Pentagon on 9/11 made this abundantly clear. The greatest loss in war is the loss of life. In a market economy, all of us are part of the same fabric. We will never know what contributions those who lost their lives on September 11 would have made to their families and their communities. In this sense, the cost of war cannot be estimated. Wars destroy factories and buildings, directly diminishing our wealth. Wars also divert resources into activities that are necessary to protect our safety, such as hiring security guards and the like, but that do not contribute to a higher standard of living.

Wars also invite bad policies. They can interfere directly with our freedom to trade with others in the world. And they often lead to higher tax rates and a disruption to monetary stability. In each of these ways—higher tax rates, the destruction of the international monetary system, and a lurch toward trade protectionism—the Vietnam War contributed directly to the end of the prosperity of the 1960s. So far, at least, these understandable impulses toward bad economic policies are being resisted.

The second threat is the failure of central banks to provide a system of predictable monetary stability. The three key central banks of the world—the Bank of Japan, the European Central Bank, and the Federal Reserve—have all admitted in one way or another that they don't know how to provide predictable monetary stability. The Fed spent the year reducing the overtight Fed Funds rate, which it controls, in a series of steps. At the beginning of the year, the Fed Funds rate was at 6.5 percent. After eleven cuts, the Fed Funds ended the year at 1.75 percent. But if 1.75 percent was the correct rate, why didn't the Fed go there directly? The answer is clear. The Board of Governors, which sets the rate, does not really know what the correct rate is. As a consequence, we have a trial and error monetary policy. The error of 2001 produced the first deflationary recession since the 1930s. The only reason we're getting away with today's discretionary monetary system is because of Mr. Greenspan's great skill and the great skill of his predecessor, Paul Volcker. Mr. Greenspan's tenure has not been error-free, but he's been quick to correct his errors. But what happens if we get somebody as head of the

Central Bank who isn't as quick to correct his errors? We could be in a fix.

Also, the lack of a monetary standard leaves a wide open space on the geopolitical board. And as you know, power hates a vacuum. I believe it is the responsibility of the United States to provide a stable currency and a standard for the world monetary system. But if we don't, somebody else will—probably the European Central Bank or, five or ten years from now, the Chinese. If that happens, the United States will suffer an enormous loss of economic power because the country that provides a monetary system will dominate the world economy. So that's one big threat.

The third biggest threat is Medicare. The risk is in making a promise—a big promise—that we can't keep. And it doesn't matter how worthy your intentions are. If you fail to deliver, you create a big mess. We're at risk of making that error with Medicare. There's no doubt that we have to reform Medicare. Adding even a limited prescription drug benefit will cost an estimated 200 billion dollars or more over the next ten years. Considering that we have a ten trillion dollar economy, 200 billion dollars over ten years is a benefit we can afford for the next ten years. But what about the ten years after that, when the Boomers start to retire? And what if the benefit becomes unlimited, and the use of prescription drugs and the cost of the program increase way beyond the estimates, as has happened in the past with Medicare?

That's when the numbers begin to get seriously very large. And what are we going to do then if we don't have the resources we need? Are we going to say sorry, we can't give you those benefits? Are we going to break the promise? I don't think so. What we'll do is raise payroll taxes because the social imperative to keep this promise will be extremely high. But if we impose massive tax increases on our economy, we will destroy economic growth. And without growth, given the demographics, there's no way Social Security or Medicare can possibly meet their obligations. So this is the mistake that could lead to a series of policy errors that could end the prosperity.

RD: *What's the solution?*

CK: There's not an obvious solution. It's going to require men and women on both sides of the political aisle to come together and find a reasonable way to provide the kind of benefits we want our senior citizens to have and at the same time to put in place the kind of reforms that will ensure that Medicare is there when the Boomers retire. There are politicians on both sides of the aisle who understand these issues. But it's incumbent upon every Baby Boomer to become an informed citizen on this issue. Because if we make a big mistake in this, we're not going to get the medical care we want, and it won't matter how good our intentions were. So we need to be engaged in this, and we need a bipartisan solution based on a realistic, if not cautious, assumption about the total costs and available funding without significant, counter-productive tax increases. If we can come up with a well-designed Medicare system, it will be a lasting legacy of the Baby Boomer generation.

One other issue also deserves attention. Baby Boomers need to take a leadership role in the repeal of the death tax. I believe this will lead to a golden era of philanthropic giving. It's venal to say that the reason people give to charities is to avoid taxes—and it's just plain not true. Here's my evidence: in the 1980s, when they cut the top tax rate from 70 percent to 28 percent, philanthropic giving grew geometrically, far faster than income. Repealing the death tax will allow our generation to engage in true charitable giving. And when we have that opportunity, I think we will surprise the world with how generous we are. It will be the hallmark of a free society to have this blossoming of privately funded philanthropic activity. If we do this successfully, it will be a legacy that Boomers can marvel at.

RD: *I'm not certain it will work that way.*

CK: I'm not either. But I'm optimistic. I'm optimistic in part because in writing the book, I gained an enormous appreciation for the ability of free people to make a better world.

RD: *I'll second that. Thank you very much.*

What does the future hold? I haven't a clue. Maybe Charles is right in his assessments, and—despite current difficulties—boom times will reassert themselves and continue until 2020. But he could be wrong. Maybe Harry S. Dent, Jr. is right, and the boom times will only continue until 2008 or 2009. Or maybe the current situation is far more serious than any of us would like to think.

One thing for sure: The future is not locked in stone. It's locked in mud. And mud, as we all know, can be very slippery indeed. My advice? Don't count on anything. Be aware. Have a Plan A and a Plan B. And don't quit your day job—at least not until you read Chapter 5.

3

The Real Deal on Image

People can say that image doesn't matter. But it does. As someone who has helped a multitude of dissatisfied people turn their careers around, I can tell you, image matters enormously. Your image influences your ability to progress professionally, to win friends, to get loans from banks, to sway opinion, and to attract the confidence and interest of others. A positive image inspires people to value your contributions and to want to give you things. So your future depends on it. To think otherwise is self-destructive. Image is crucial.

Image incorporates far more than looks. Behavior, speech, manners, body language, and overall confidence are of primary importance.

But initially, what matters most is appearance. Because when it comes to making an impression—and particularly a first impression—you've got very little time.

How little? At least two books maintain that you've got five minutes. (The two books: *The First Five Minutes* by Norman King, and *The First Five Minutes* by Mary Mitchell with John Corr. As many authors have learned to their distress, you can't copyright titles.)

My experience suggests that five minutes is too generous. Camille Lavington and Stephanie Losee agree. They're the authors of *You've Only Got Three Seconds.*

But I have to say, three seconds strikes me as an unfairly fleeting moment. I estimate that, as a general rule, you've got about one or two minutes to make a good impression. So when I heard that Nicholas Boothman had written a book called *How to Make People Like You in 90 Seconds or Less,* I thought I'd found an author who saw things my way.

But guess what? In an interview published in the *New York Times,* Boothman states definitively that "We decide within two seconds how we're going to react to someone. We're hard-wired to make snap judgments."

I hate to think that it's all over in the blink of an eye. But if he's right, it behooves us all to use that moment to maximum advantage. The first step is to recognize that the process of sizing someone up begins before a word is spoken. It begins with your appearance.

Naturally, heredity has something to do with that, as do exercise and diet. The fitter you look, the better. That's a given. But my concern, as a public relations expert, is in how you present yourself. That's something you can control, even if you could have done better in the gene department . . . even if you're fighting a lifelong aversion to the gym . . . and even if you're over fifty.

Once you've crossed that great divide, you no longer have youth on your side. You may be glowing in good health and sex appeal and money. But youth, which enhances appearance like nothing else, has fled. So presentation becomes more important than ever.

Is this shallow? No. It's realistic. Begin with clothing. Being well dressed—which is to say, dressing in a way that is both appropriate and flattering—is only a small part of your image. But it provides an important base.

Clothing Matters

Clothes never shut up.
Alison Lurie

"Clothes are inevitable," wrote James Laver, author of *Style in Costume*. "They are nothing less than the furniture of the mind made visible." They broadcast everything about us: where we shop, where we live, class, profession, politics, and more. They are neither incidental nor irrelevant, and paying attention to them is worth the time, the effort, and even the money.

I recently talked to a man who, as provost at a nearby community college, interviewed a number of Ph.D.s for a tenure-track position. One particular candidate was well spoken and his academic record was excellent. Nevertheless he made a bad impression because, unlike the other candidates, all of whom dressed up, he appeared in front of the committee wearing jeans and a plaid shirt. Now, colleges are notoriously casual places, and many professors teach in outfits just like that. But an interview is not a class, and ultimately, the feeling was that he hadn't shown respect. Needless to say, he didn't get the job.

He didn't stop to think that clothes always carry a message. As Alison Lurie writes in *The Language of Clothes*, "even when we say nothing our clothes are talking noisily to everyone who sees us . . . We can lie in the language of dress, or try to tell the truth; but unless we are naked and bald it is impossible to be silent."

I try to dress with style and dignity and, if possible, comfort. Unfortunately, I was born without a fashion sense. I don't trust myself to choose a tie, no less to identify the right fabric for a suit or to know what's in style this season. I have no idea. So I rely on others.

But before I share their advice with you, I have to backtrack.

A Confession

Some men cheat on their wives. I do not.

Some men cheat on their taxes. Not me: Who wants to risk an encounter with the IRS?

But far be it from me to throw the first stone, for I have cheated too. Through no fault of theirs, I have been two-timing my haberdashers. My first haberdasher, Marvin Piland, is a former music teacher with a second career in retail. When I met him, he was in charge of personal shopping at the Men's Fifth Avenue Club at Saks in New York City. That's where I came to rely on his flawless taste and his ability to spruce up even the most difficult cases. I worked with him for many years, and I still do.

Then, about five years ago, I moved to Connecticut, where I met Bill Mitchell. He owns two clothing stores. His store in Westport was closer to me than Saks, and so I began to buy suits from him. I kept my allegiance to Marvin, with whom I continued to do business. But I never did summon up the courage to tell either Marvin or Bill about the other.

I'd like to remedy that now. Here's part of my interview with Marvin Piland, who has saved me from many a sartorial mistake.

MARVIN PILAND

RD: *Why is it important to have an advisor like yourself?*

MP: A hundred years ago, a young man's father would take him to the tailor. It was something men did together, like fishing or hunting. You went to your father's tailor and you learned about clothing. It was considered manly knowledge, something you needed to acquire. Today, men see it as something that smacks of not being manly. So it's ignored. Also, the pace of contemporary life can be so demanding, that you have to limit what you're focusing on. Most men focus on career—not dress. Then when a man finally achieves a certain position, somebody will say, "Hey, you've got to pull yourself together." And he doesn't have a clue how to do it. That's when they will come to places like the Men's Fifth Avenue Club.

RD: *How do you think a man over fifty should dress?*

MP: First of all, he should not dress like a thirty-year-old. He should look good for his age. He should have a style that projects confidence in what he does. In today's world, it should be done in an easy way. You don't want to be too uptight or too obviously dressed. The clothes should not call attention

to themselves. Quality should be evident. They should be un-
contrived and low key, but well maintained. You want to look
pulled together, with quality and comfort.

RD: *Does a man's wardrobe change as he gets older?*

MP: It should. For example: Fit is the most important part of buying a suit. Our bodies change over time. As much as we don't
want to admit it, our waistline will expand. Our shoulders
will become more rounded. So you may be wearing a soft-
shouldered garment in your thirties. When you get older,
you may want to go to a traditional suit to flatter your body
and add more definition. You can keep the same style but
modify the silhouette to give shape and structure.

RD: *What are the worst mistakes a man can make?*

MP: Well, the first is where he wears his belt. If you foolishly want
to keep a thirty-four-inch waist and wear the belt lower with
that tummy plumping out, you're on your own.

Another mistake is dyeing your hair to look younger. That
is one of the worst mistakes a man can make, especially if he
does it himself. I have seen very few examples where it's been
done well. Coloring your hair requires a true professional
and frequent care. It should never be obvious—and it usually
is. Also, you don't want to wear anything that will date you.
For example, a wingtip shoe is just not in fashion now. You're
better off wearing a cap toe shoe or a plain toe shoe. It's still
traditional and conservative but it has moved along with the
times.

RD: *What steps can a man take to improve his appearance?*

MP: Treat your body well. Plan and implement an exercise program that works for you. Exercising doesn't mean building a
he-man physique. It means having energy, endurance, and
firm muscle tone. Good nutrition and good health habits
also contribute to a sense of well-being. And take care of
your teeth. As we get into our fifties, teeth yellow with age.

This is a sure sign of growing older but it can be corrected easily.

RD: *How important is it to buy expensive clothes?*

MP: One of the worst mistakes a man can make is trying to find a bargain. Good quality clothes hang on the body better, and this is extremely important as we age. As our bodies change, we need clothes that are well constructed, have good balance to them, and are properly tailored. I think that's very important.

I don't think it's important to the advancement of a career that you buy a status symbol brand. What is important is to buy clothing that fits you properly.

Also, less is more. It's better to have three better suits than five medium priced suits. Better suits are going to last over time. In the end, clothing of good quality will be the better bargain.

RD: *How have business styles changed?*

MP: Obviously we are more casual. I think Casual Friday is going to be here for the rest of my career, even though it has created enormous insecurity, especially in men. Women understand separates. Men do not. You have to think about dressing, and most men don't want to do that. They don't want to worry about what goes with what. When you have a blue suit and a blue shirt, you can buy four different ties to go with it, and you're set. But with separates and sportswear, you've got to consider shades and textures and the correct shoes, etc., etc. It's more complicated and time consuming. Quite frankly, men have been confused about it. In that respect, it's helped our consultation business. Men are coming to us and saying, "Help, how do I do this?"

On the other hand, I do think that, in a distressed economy, we are coming back to more formal attire in order to keep a competitive edge. That means dressing with care.

RD: *What should you wear to an interview?*

MP: You've got to know the business you're going into. You can't lose by wearing a suit, a shirt, and a tie. It doesn't have to be a formal blue suit with a starched white shirt. That can make you look a little uptight. If you're going into an informal area like advertising, you might consider wearing a solid blazer or a sport coat with wool trousers and a crisp, well-laundered shirt. If you're not sure, it's always better to be slightly over-dressed than underdressed. Also, grooming is important. When I'm interviewing someone, I look at their hands to see how clean they are. I look to see if their shoes are polished.

RD: *The traditional advice for how to dress on the job is to dress for the position you hope to obtain. How do you feel about that?*

MP: After fifty, you should dress with an ease and comfort that show quality and confidence. Forget trying to convince someone that you can do the job through the way you dress. Self-conscious dressing isn't going to work.

RD: *What about colors? I read an interesting book by Alison Lurie called* The Language of Clothes. *She talks about the meaning of clothes. She says that, in Great Britain, people tend to dress according to the principle of camouflage. In the country, they wear green and brown. In urban areas, they wear black, white, navy, and shades of gray. I've kept my eye out, and I think it's true here too. In the city, men mostly wear blue and gray.*

MP: They do create a sense of power. I was at the theater last night. I noticed many brown suits but not one man in a brown suit created a strong impression. I don't want to kill the brown suit business, but brown tends to pull the color out of the face. It doesn't create strength.

RD: *What about ties?*

MP: Ties should not call attention to themselves. You want to look at a man's face. When you have a bright orange tie with green spots on it, you're looking at the tie, and the man be-comes secondary or, even worse comes off as a buffoon. A tie should be quiet, understated, and coordinated with his suit.

RD: *What about bow ties?*

MP: Bow ties are dated. I'm not saying they won't come back but right now they're a little old-fashioned.

RD: *And suspenders?*

MP: They hold your pants up. I recommend them for that, but they should be worn with a jacket. They're very comfortable. With suspenders—the English call them braces—you can wear your trousers a little easier and you don't have that belt cutting you off in the middle. It's a matter of personal style. I wear them myself.

RD: *What about other accessories like handkerchiefs?*

MP: Unless he has a very sartorial style, a serious businessman in today's world doesn't wear them. Younger, more youthful suits—Dolce & Gabbana, Paul Smith, Gucci—don't require handkerchiefs. They have a more contemporary look. For a younger man, a handkerchief would be an anachronism. For a man who's secure in his style and has done it all his life, it would be fine.

RD: *So it's okay if you're over fifty, but if you're under fifty, you're going to look . . .*

MP: . . . like a dandy.

RD: *What about cuff links?*

MP: Cuff links add a little flash to the outfit and a look of afflu-ence. French cuff shirts offer a more mature, established look, and one that is always in good taste—with the appropriate cuff links, of course. No sparklers and no Texas-sized designs.

RD: *I think that covers it. Thanks, Marvin.*

BILL MITCHELL

Not only does Bill Mitchell have great taste in clothes (I think even Marvin would approve), he runs a highly successful family business that is notable for the degree of personal service it offers. Mitchell's was founded by Bill's ninety-six-year-old father. It now includes two stores and several hundred employees. Here's what he has to say—as a clothier and as a businessman.

RD: *Do you find that people over fifty make mistakes in presenting themselves?*

BM: Yes. Their dress code is not with it. Women tend to be up to speed. But men are not up to current fashion and standards. They've got to be much more in tune with current fashions.

For example, you know how lapels come and go? Several years ago they were wider, then they were narrower. The whole silhouette of a suit or a jacket will change every couple of years. Rarely do I see a man who's older who's up to the moment with fashion.

RD: *Obviously you're going to notice that because you have an eye that is specifically geared to that. But is a guy who runs an insurance company going to see that?*

BM: Maybe not. But a lot of CEOs who run major companies come to us for direction, and because of that, I think they will notice.

RD: *If a man over fifty comes in and he wants to present himself in the best possible way for a job interview, what do you tell him?*

BM: First of all, I find out where his interests lay and who his employer is. Find out if he's going to Wall Street or General Electric or a bank. We're pretty tuned in to the dress code of various companies. If we don't know, we'll call human resources and find out. So, number one, we do the homework for the client. And number two, I always say, "Put that suit on." Now, if it's a very casual company, and someone goes a little too dressed up, that's not good either. But times are changing, and with some of these companies, the pendulum is swinging back again to dressing up. Most times, for job interviews, it's better to err on the side of overdressing as opposed to underdressing.

RD: *Are there differences in the way companies expect their employees to dress?*

BM: There really are. They can be anywhere from very formal to 100 percent casual. Some of the more conservative employers like Bank of New York have remained dressier. At NBC Sports, it's all casual, although the president of NBC always wears a suit. Greenwich Capital is a huge investment firm and you can wear jeans at that company. At Bear Stearns they changed from casual to suits. Because of the unsteady economy over the last year or so, some of these people have given the edict out to their associates to stop the casual dress and go back to suits for men and the counterpart for women. All of a sudden, they had better start looking professional and being in the business of serious business. The economy has forced them to make the shift.

One of our clients is the head of human resources at a major company in New York—I'm not at liberty to tell you the name of it. She was shopping here in January. I was quizzing her about this dress stuff and she said, "You know, my chairman and I just had breakfast and we wished we could undo what we did five years ago in going casual. It became a nightmare." Casual dress was never really defined. What does it mean? Sweaters? Sneakers? Khakis or dress slacks? Or jeans? All of a sudden these companies were not reflecting who they were. And then they pulled people like me into seminars. We've tried to give these companies some guidance as to what to wear. It was difficult because naturally I'm not running General Electric or IBM. It's ultimately their decision. But my philosophy is that your success should be reflected in your clothes. The better you dress, the better you feel, and the better you feel, the greater your success. A lot of people judge a book by its cover.

RD: *It seems to me a man can't go wrong with a navy blue or gray suit, assuming it's not out of style.*

BM: That's correct.

RD: *But women have greater choice.*

BM: Yes. So it's even tougher for women. A woman is more likely to consider her own palette, her hair and the color of the skin. Fifteen or twenty years ago, I might have told a woman to go with something in a gray or blue, but those days are gone. Today, something in toned-down red or beige could be good-looking and appropriate. Very subtle prints are acceptable. In the last two years, the career woman has started to dress up again. But there's not a clear direction, nor has there been one in the last few years. For women in corporate America, it really is negotiable.

RD: *Do small items make a difference in creating an image?*

BM: You bet. For a man, a tie can make all the difference in the world. For a woman, a pair of shoes can make the outfit. And it can also bust it.

And for men, a small item like a belt is the last thing that he will think about. Several years go by before most men buy a new belt. And it will start to fray. The width of the belt will change with the style of the suit.

RD: *What's the style of belts now?*

BM: Medium width. Ten, twelve years ago, narrow belts were in style. Then it went to thick. It's a middle-of-the-road thing now.

RD: *Bill, you're an employer. Aside from dress, what are the most important mistakes you see people over fifty making?*

BM: I can tell you in a nutshell: They resist change. For example, you and I both know that there are always new ways to reach a client. In my industry, there's been a huge change in the last few years. There's more personal contact. You've got to make people feel special. The merchandise we sell is the same as Saks or Neiman Marcus, so service is the only edge we have. My shtick is to go beyond the customer's expectations in terms of service. We'll hem a dress and deliver it three hours later to Kennedy Airport, or fit a suit at seven o'clock in the morning at a client's home.

But I've noticed that, as people get older, they are less willing to go that extra mile. They don't want to try something different. Some know they've got to do it to survive but they're not eager to jump in. Younger people will do it in a heartbeat. They're not set in their ways. Some of our older people don't seem to think they've got to change the way they do things. In my business if you don't, you're not going to survive.

It's easy to train and coach new, young, energetic blood. If you're over fifty, you've got to be flexible. You've got to be smart, you've got to love what you do, and you have to go way beyond ordinary expectations.

RD: *And you find that older employees resist this more?*

BM: They sure do.

RD: *A word to the wise. Thanks, Bill.*

A Word to the Women

My wife can tell you: I know nothing about women's clothing. But Susan Ratliff has a background in fashion, and she does. She has worked for Calvin Klein, I. Magnin's, and now Barneys, an upscale specialty store in Manhattan where she is a personal shopper. I asked her a few questions.

SUSAN RATLIFF

RD: *What are the most important aspects of appearance for a woman over fifty?*

SR: Less is more after age fifty. Skirts shouldn't be too short or too tight. Hair shouldn't be too long or too big. Nails shouldn't be too long or too red. They should be short, lightly polished, well manicured. The key issue is grooming. Over age fifty a woman should wear light makeup. Heavy makeup is a mistake. Shoes should be polished and in good shape. Same for handbags and briefcases. And clothes should look pressed and pristine.

RD: *If a woman over fifty is on the job market, and particularly if she is going for an interview, what should she wear?*

SR: It differs from industry to industry. In advertising or entertaining or fashion, wearing a wool suit in September or October with bare legs is acceptable. With a Manolo Blahnik shoe, it would be considered very chic. But in a law firm or a Wall Street office or most of the business world, a woman who wasn't wearing hose would not be considered properly groomed. So there are subtle differences from industry to industry.

RD: *Is it important for a woman to wear a suit?*

SR: Again, it depends. If you're going to work at an advertising agency, maybe you could get away with a nice sweater set and a pair of pants, but that's not as polished or put together as a suit. My clients who work on Wall Street or in business will wear pants to work but I have noticed they still like skirt suits.

In the 1980s the power suit was all important. In the 1990s people were experimenting. Women decided that they didn't necessarily need that power suit to feel professional. But honestly, most of the women executives that I know still wear a suit. And maybe they don't wear the Armani wool crepe suit anymore. Maybe they branched out and are doing things with a little bit more flare. But I have noticed that even my friends who are in the fashion world at senior levels still wear a jacket if they have an important presentation. It makes them feel put together.

It seems to me that for the professional woman, a suit is still the best look, assuming it's nicely tailored and not too short. If you can afford to splurge on an expensive suit, I would encourage it. A good black suit can take you from day to evening to the theater to dinner.

RD: *I don't want to get out of my depth, so I'm only going to ask you two more questions. How important is color?*

SR: Well, it's important. But it depends where you are. In Florida and the south, or even Texas, lighter colors work better than dark ones. In New York and other urban areas, we tend to wear black and gray and navy. Darker colors work best, unless it's high summer. Then I recommend neutral colors or black with a lot of white.

RD: *Any other advice for women?*

SR: Use personal shoppers! They are a store's best kept secret, and they are free of charge. Personal shoppers get to know their best clients so well, they pull things for them before they even hit the floor. In fact, the great things never hit the floor at all.

RD: *That's useful information. Thanks, Susan.*

How to Dress: Dilenschneider's Guide to Fashion Over Fifty

With advisors like Marvin and Bill, I have finally figured out, at this late stage in life, how to dress. These are the essentials:

- Cultivate a personal style. By the time you've reached your fifties, you should have a sense of what works for you and what does not. Go with that. But don't let your style get mired in the past. Don't be like one of those people still sporting tie-dye, two generations after Woodstock . . . or football shoulders fifteen years after Ronald Reagan . . . or yellow power ties when their moment is long gone.
- Keep up to date. Read *GQ* or *Vogue,* at least occasionally. Make certain you've got at least one outfit that fits with both your personal style and this year's fashions, and wear it for important meetings.
- Eschew passing fads. If teenagers are wearing it, you should not. Also, when items that were stylish in your youth, such as bell bottoms, micro-minis, or leisure suits return, as they inevitably do, shun them. If you were old enough to wear it the first time around, you're too old to wear it now. Similarly, under no circumstances should you display your midriff, get a tattoo, or pierce your body anyplace but the earlobes.
- Pay attention to belts, shoes, watches, and other accessories, and keep them up-to-date.
- Your briefcase or handbag is an important part of your image. Make certain it reflects your success.
- If you're wearing a suit, or even a shirt and tie, remember: the tie is not an accessory. It is the capstone of your outfit and must be chosen with infinite care. My best advice: Get help. (I rely on three people: Marvin, Bill, and my wife.)
- Remember that clothes, like batteries, eventually run out of juice, which means that even classic items need to be replaced from time to time. That navy blue blazer may look, to your eyes, as fresh as the day you bought it back in the era of George Bush the First. To everyone else, it looks tired. And that microscopic little spot you think no one notices? Think again.
- Quality counts. Buy the best clothing you can afford.
- Grooming matters. If you're a man, you can get away with neat and clean. If you're a woman, you probably need to do more. Unfair? Of course. But the truth is, unless you're in a noncorporate environment, makeup, however minimal, is es-

sential. And if you live in New York or other large cities, you may also be expected to have a manicure.

- When in doubt, seek professional help. Every department store has personal shoppers who are more than willing to spend time with you.

The Substance Beneath the Surface

Clothing speaks volumes and has a great impact on your image. But let's face it: Image is more than appearance. In today's fast paced world, if people are going to take you as a serious person, they look for substance. And that substance has to be solid. It can't be how you look or your style of speech. It can't be your wardrobe or your car or even your title. It's got to be content: the content of your character, as Martin Luther King Jr. said, and the content of your mind.

I had a client who struck me as successful, attractive, and utterly superficial . . . until he started to talk about Samuel Johnson, the great English lexicographer. He said that Dr. Johnson was a great thinker and philosopher who was not a wealthy man because he gave everything away. That comment led into a thoughtful conversation about the complexities and importance of giving. And suddenly, my client gained stature. People saw him now as a person of ideas—not as the guy in the Armani suit. By revealing his substance, he improved his image.

Image gets you in the door: that's why it's important. Substance keeps you in the game, no matter how old you are.

Sophia Loren, no slouch in the looks department, said it well: "There is a fountain of youth: it is your mind, your talents, the creativity you bring to your life and the lives of the people you love. When you learn to tap this source, you will have truly defeated age."

No one knows that better than Letitia Baldrige. During the thousand days of the Kennedy administration, she was Jacqueline Kennedy's social secretary. She's hobnobbed with the best, the brightest, and the most beautiful. At age seventy-six, she has published eighteen books and is editor of a monthly newsletter,

Executive Advantage. And—by the way—she looks great. But she also knows what really matters.

Here's a transcript of my telephone interview with her.

LETITIA BALDRIGE

RD: *I wondered if you could address the question of what issues come up after fifty.*

LB: Sure. The main questions that people worry about after fifty are: Do I look old? Is my mind slipping? Am I forgetful? I think when people get to be fifty they become almost paranoid about the age situation. Are they looking young enough? Are they acting young enough? Do they have a young enough car? Do they have a good enough job? And if they've been passed over or shunted aside and forced to take on a new career, is it prestigious enough? Or are people going to compare it to the one before and say well, he or she can't do any better than that? So it's a very tough time.

You have to have self-confidence. You have to keep telling yourself look, I've lived these many years, and I've learned all kinds of things, I've accomplished all kinds of things, and I am terrific.

RD: *What are the worst mistakes that people over fifty make in presenting themselves?*

LB: Trying to look too young. Talking about their diets. Talking about their face lifts and their bellies, showing off their abs. This self-adulation, this terrible thing we have about physical appearance and the gym and everything, is awful. We have become boring and obsessed. And it's unbecoming.

RD: *A men's clothier at Saks told me that one of the worst mistakes a man can make is to dye his hair.*

LB: I think that to wear a rug is even worse.

RD: *But what about a woman?*

LB: Since the beginning of time, women have dyed their hair. Back in the dark ages, women dyed their hair. It's expected of us. It is not of men.

RD: *What are the best steps that people over fifty can take to improve their image?*

LB: Well, do things that you haven't done before. Read. Read great books. Read great plays. And take great pride in doing this. Take pride in becoming a museum hound and learning about the history of art. Take pride in learning about American history. There are any number of things which have nothing to do with earning money or looking beautiful but which have everything to do with looking beautiful inside.

RD: *What about conversation? Are there ways people can specifically improve their conversation?*

LB: First of all, realize it needs improvement. Secondly, your conversation improves if you are well read, if you are stimulated, if you keep up with the news. If you suddenly drop the *Wall Street Journal* and then you drop the *Daily News* because you get the *New York Times,* if you start dropping all these papers, which I see people do from the age of fifty-five on, you're losing a tremendous sense of the tempo of the times. If you add to your reading and add to your knowledge, you have sparkling things to talk about.

RD: *Have you seen people over fifty or fifty-five change careers or shift the focus of their career in an interesting way?*

LB: Oh, sure. I saw one man leave a very important advertising agency job and go up to Salem, Massachusetts, and buy a boatyard and start making special boats and selling them all over the world. People do change, and if they're smart and bright and full of energy, they usually make a success.

RD: *Do you think that women face particular issues over fifty?*

LB: Oh, they do. Some women predicate their whole lives on the man they're seen with, the man who's "taking care of them," the man who's paying the bills, the man who gets them to the chic resorts for the industry meetings. Those women ought to wise up. If she's fifty, her husband may be looking else-where, in another direction, and she should be prepared to have a good life on her own and to branch out and get her professional life in order. She should not go to pot physi-cally—nobody should go to pot physically—but there's a great difference between going to pot physically and being obsessed with one's beauty and spending all one's money getting the wrinkles taken care of and the flab suctioned out.

RD: *Let me change the subject. I just went to the library and took out your first book,* Roman Candle.

LB: Ha! My God!

RD: *You begin the book by quoting your grandmother's advice.*

LB: Oh, my grandmother. Always giving me advice.

RD: *Here's what she said. I'm holding the book in my hand right now so I can tell you exactly what it says. You wrote, "Tish, just remember, if you marry the right man, it's a fortunate accident. It's accidental if you pick the proper man, and it's sheer luck if he falls in love with you at the same time. But in* everything *else in life, you get what you work for. Dream your dreams, set your sights, and go out after all of them." Do you still agree with that quote?*

LB: Well, yes. Absolutely. Do it all. Never get stuck in a rut. Do it all.

RD: *Do you think that after fifty a person should reassess in some way?*

LB: No! Keep going after it. Do the things you haven't been able to do. Get it done. Just say, listen, as long as I'm still on my feet, as long as I can still perambulate, as long as my brain still works, go for it!

RD: *I couldn't agree with you more.*

In sum, what makes for an appealing image? An attractive appearance; an easy manner; confidence; and a lively, expansive mind. The people I interviewed in this chapter have those qualities in spades.

4

Time to Change

For several years, I have had the privilege of addressing groups of people at the Learning Annex of New York. I do this because I want to understand what's going on in America, and I don't think I can accomplish that by spending all my time with corporate executives. At the Learning Annex, where the classes range in size from thirty to over a hundred students, I interact with a much broader slice of the population. These people come from all walks of life and every part of the globe. They're all ages, all sexes, all colors. As far as I can tell, they have three things in common. First, every one of them managed to pick up a Learning Annex catalog, probably from one of those ubiquitous dispensers you see on the street. Second, all of them are yearning for change, especially at work. And third, they're hoping that someone will come along and tell them what to do.

I remember a woman in one of my classes who worked for a large jewelry store. In a room full of people wearing jeans and sweatshirts, she was dressed as elegantly as you can imagine. She sat there throughout the class and at the end asked a series of precise, focused questions, none of which had anything to do with my lecture. They were about how she could change her life. She encouraged feedback, and it was interesting to watch her. There she was, in a group of people she would probably never see again, getting fifteen or twenty opinions on questions of great importance to her. She clearly saw the people in the class as resources, and she wanted to use them to best advantage.

Like everyone else in that room, she was dissatisfied. The people who sign up for my classes assume that they are going to spend eight to ten hours a day at a job, and they want to enjoy it. Instead, they feel frustrated or bored. They don't like their bosses or their co-workers. They feel unable to use their abilities and imagination. They complain that there's no opportunity to move up. Yet sometimes they're not even skilled at what they do. Eventually, they say, enough. In their souls, in their hearts, and in their stomachs they know that it's time to make a change. They see a green field shimmering in the distance and they say to themselves, that's where I want to be. I've got to find a way.

Since you're reading this book and this chapter, you may have that same visceral urge. You don't need to be convinced. You don't need to be pushed out. You've already got one foot out the door.

Or you may be unsure, stymied, frozen in your discontent. You dread Monday mornings but tell yourself that things could be worse. You wonder how you got into this situation, and you count the years to retirement like a prisoner in an old movie crossing off the days on a calendar. You rationalize that there are times when doing nothing is the smartest move you can make.

Actually, that's sometimes true. If you've got six months to go before your pension is vested, you'd be foolish to quit. But usually, it's better to take the initiative and explore other options.

To do that effectively, you've got to be ruthlessly honest with yourself. You've got to inventory your strengths and recognize your weaknesses. And you've got to acknowledge the possibility that if you're dissatisfied, you're probably not doing a bang-up job. Your boss may be as unhappy with you as you are with him.

Impossible? Too often, people who have lost their jobs tell me that they didn't see it coming. That means only one thing: They weren't paying attention.

Red Flags

An article by Joann S. Lublin in the *Wall Street Journal* proposed ten indications that a layoff is about to occur. Here are my ten indicators on a related topic: How can you tell when your own employment is on the line?

1. Your boss is on your case all the time. This can happen to anyone. No matter how competent and helpful you are, you can't seem to get a break. There are all kinds of reasons for this. The boss may be insecure. The boss may have it in for women, or men, or gays, and if you fall into one of those categories, you've had it. Or maybe he dislikes you personally. It could be anything. One thing's for sure: if you have a miserable relationship with your boss and there's no way to work around it, you've got to get out of there.

Keep in mind, too, that sometimes the boss is purposely harassing you, either because he thinks it is an effective technique or because he hopes he can convince you to quit. For instance, at a major art company based in the Middle West, the CEO, whom I'll call Joe Reynolds, went after a half dozen of his people virtually every day. He was constantly asking for reports, setting unrealistic deadlines, standing over them, calling to ask for progress reports, monitoring when they came and went, and more. He claimed that he was trying to stimulate creativity. My suspicion was that he was trying to reduce his head count. He wasn't personally targeting anyone. But there were significant cross-pressures in his company and he needed to lower expenses.

In one sense, the technique worked. A number of people quit in frustration. But in another sense, it backfired. Several workers took to creating a whole range of ploys to drive him crazy. For example, one man arranged for calls that would pull Reynolds away from the office so that he wouldn't be there to hover over the time clock. Other people created bogus projects to distract his attention.

All of this led to internal dissension and the eventual fracturing of what was once a fine department.

Did Reynolds reduce head count? Absolutely. But along the

way his productivity suffered and he created a level of bitterness that didn't have to be there.

I knew another guy like Reynolds. He was an oil company executive who made a practice of intimidating his people in order to get rid of them. Over a two-year period, ten superb people left because he was constantly on their case. One time, he publicly ridiculed one of his employees because he subscribed to *Mother Jones*. The poor guy had to defend himself for reading the magazine. Needless to say, it didn't matter what his reasons were. His head was already on the block.

2. You've been told that you're in trouble. Your annual evaluation indicates need for improvement. You've been put on probation. Or you've been told to take a refresher course. There's only one way to interpret that, and it's not good: Somebody up there doesn't think your performance is adequate.

I've watched people twist themselves into knots trying to come up with other interpretations. They're wasting their time. Your boss would not have initiated this distressing conversation without thinking carefully about it. It's possible that your boss has decided, perhaps for reasons of conscience, to give you one more chance.

You have two choices, and probably you should go for both of them. You can throw yourself into your work by doing everything you possibly can to be successful, thus overcoming the crisis of the moment. And you can begin looking for a new job.

I'm reminded of a man I'll call Gary whom I ran into several months ago in a club in Greenwich, Connecticut. His boss had just told him that his work was substandard and that he had one month to turn it around. He asked my advice. I said, Gary, do whatever you can but understand that the boss would not have told you this had he not given the whole matter considerable thought. He is wondering whether you have the long-term abilities to benefit the organization. If I were you, I'd begin preparing a résumé now.

Gary couldn't accept that. He decided to stick it out. As a result, he gradually became ostracized in the workplace. After the boss let it be known that he had given Gary an ultimatum, his colleagues shied away. He was excluded from meetings. People who used to go to coffee with him wouldn't see him, and he and his wife were shunned when it came to entertaining in the evening. For eight or nine months, he stayed in the company. Less and less information came his way every day, and his responsibilities were gradually eroded. Eventually the stress and the isolation caught up with him. His health began to suffer and he and his wife started to have harsh words. He thought he had failed. In fact, he hadn't failed. He'd just been pushed out. When he finally understood that, he resigned and ended the pain. But it took him longer than it should have.

Was he a hero in sticking it out? I don't think so. Once he saw that his efforts to improve the situation were going nowhere, he should have faced the truth—never an easy thing to do—and moved on.

3. You're asked to provide detailed reports about time or expenses. This is an ominous sign if you've been singled out. But even if the edict is department-wide, you need to be cautious. Increased scrutiny is a phenomenon that is rarely initiated by the accounting department. Normally it's initiated by a boss who wants to use the accounting vehicle as a way to get at you. The boss generally feels that you have wasted time or inflated expenses. You may be 100 percent innocent of this accusation. It doesn't matter. The fact is that once his suspicions have been aroused, you're guilty until proven innocent.

You have one line of defense: you have to show results for the time you're putting in. You have to show that you're highly productive, that you're bringing money to the bottom line for the company, and that your expense report (or time sheet) is clean as a whistle. Trust me on this: Most time and money reports are not clean. People cheat a little, here and there. Better make sure you don't.

Also, before you jump to the conclusion that you're the only person being scrutinized, find out whether that's the case. Simply ask, are you requiring everyone to do this? If the answer is no, you have the right to ask why you've been singled out. Tell them that you want to understand the situation so that you can address it, and raise it in a constructive letter to the head of the Human Resources department. You don't want to create a problem for yourself by being a corporate malcontent. But you do want to ask for evenness and fairness. That's what the workplace is supposed to be all about.

4. You have difficulty gaining access to the boss. Your efforts to schedule meetings fail. You can't get your boss on the phone. When you run into him in the hallway, he's in a hurry. You feel continually snubbed. Meanwhile, you learn that he's having lunch with your colleagues.

There are times when trying to get to the boss means dealing with intimidation. If that's the case with your boss, you have to find a way to cope with his personality, however autocratic it may be. If you can't find a way to communicate with leadership, you can assume you're not in good standing.

For instance, at one of the largest companies in the world, a public relations person was hired without the knowledge of the boss. Unfortunately, when he was introduced to top management, the chemistry couldn't have been worse. Halfway through the meeting, the boss turned on his heel and never spoke to him again. The PR person had no access other than the boss' secretary. When that secretary saw that the boss didn't like him, she froze him out too.

The public relations person had to leave. The boss is still there.

5. You've got a new boss. Bosses come and go with increasing frequency these days. Regardless of the circumstances, a new boss is a threat because he inevitably wants to bring in his own people. If your new boss doesn't seek you out, seems uninterested in getting to know you, and shows no inclination to discuss goals and strategies, you could be history.

But you've got a responsibility too. Don't hide in the corner waiting for the new boss to come to you. The best approach to step forward and tell the boss you want to do whatever you can to help. And then demonstrate that.

Many years ago at a large food company in Minneapolis, a new boss came in with a reputation for being extraordinarily tough. One of the employees, a woman I'll call Andrea, literally hid in her office in fear of the new broom. After about eight weeks, she started to relax. She thought if she just did her job and kept her head down, everything would be fine. Not long after that, the boss came along and said, Andrea, I haven't had the chance to meet you. I always wondered why you never extended yourself to me. I've formed my team in the meantime and we're moving ahead. Unfortunately, there is no place for you.

Andrea lost more than her job. Ultimately she had to change not just employer but her career because the Minneapolis market was small and the range of possibilities for what she did was limited.

The moral of the story: Don't make the boss come to you.

6. You're out of the loop. You find out about key meetings after they occur, essential memos don't come your way, and when you complain, you're assured that it was an accident. If this happens more than once, it's no oversight. It's policy.

In a Midwestern oil company, the boss reflected his displeasure with people by not inviting them to meetings—and then by questioning them about the substance of the meeting after it had taken place. It was a set-up, intended to embarrass. And it worked. At least one individual I know, not having a clue about what went on in the meeting, tried to fake it and made a fool out of himself.

In another case, a writer at a major television studio was never given the information he needed to complete his assignments. When he tried to get it, he was blocked and told it was confidential. In fact, his boss just didn't like him. He was essentially testing the writer, who theoretically could have searched out the data on his own. For one reason or another, he didn't. He failed in assignment after assignment and was dismissed from the company.

7. Your boss goes directly to your subordinates. This variation on being out of the loop occurs when, instead of talking to you about what needs to be done and allowing you to delegate, your boss goes directly to the people on your team—without consulting you. You start relying on your assistant to alert you to new developments. Or your subordinates start receiving raises, promotions, and assignments without any input from you. Like the military, most organizations have a chain of command to ensure order. When that chain of command is disrupted, especially from the top down, it is as clear an indication as you can get that your time is running out.

More typically, the breach of protocol works the other way around: a subordinate bypasses you and goes directly to your supervisor. This is also a dangerous situation, as the movie *Donnie Brasco* illustrates. In that movie, Johnny Depp, who plays the lead, bypasses his boss and mentor, mobster Al Pacino, and talks directly to the head of the Mafia about opening up operations in Florida. Pacino, feeling cut out, complains. But it's too late. Depp claims disingenuously that the Mafia leader came to him, and Pacino is marginalized.

8. Your boss asks you to do unreasonable or irrelevant tasks, often in out-of-the-way places. Pick up a visiting dignitary at midnight? Attend a nonemergency meeting on Thanksgiving Day? Once upon a time, your boss wanted to be on your good side and would not have considered mistreating you in these ways. Now, he doesn't care. He'll ask anything.

The *Wall Street Journal* cautions that even being asked to run the company charity drive may be an ominous sign. After all, prestigious as that assignment may sound, the chances are that it is irrelevant to the business you're in (unless you work for a nonprofit). Similarly, there is nothing worse than being asked to do research on projects which are promptly shelved. One or two assignments along those lines may mean you're being eased out.

Another warning sign is being asked to travel to a distant location only to find out that there is little or no purpose to the meeting. This happens all the time. It's a way for bosses to get people out of the way without confronting them.

An extreme variation on this technique comes masked in the shape of a job transfer. The FBI in J. Edgar Hoover's day was famous for exiling its unwanted agents to Billings, Montana, and other remote places. These days, it happens like this: Your boss announces that there's an opportunity in Fargo, North Dakota, and he'd like you to go there with your family. Unfortunately, the company can't pay the cost of moving. How do you feel about it? The message is clear.

I have noticed that when these things happen, some people wonder if the problem is their age. It may well be. But believe me, you'll never be able to prove it. Lots of people think that the laws and regulations of the Equal Employment Opportunity Commission (EEOC) are there to prevent this. The truth is, smart employers and their lawyers know how to get around them.

9. Your perks start to evaporate. Everyone else troops off to a conference in Marrakesh but your presence is not required. The down-time you used to receive between major projects evaporates. When you're lucky enough to be assigned additional staff, they're never the best candidates. You're told these are cost-saving measures. In fact, the powers that be don't want you to have certain perks—the car, the club, expense account lunches, and so on—because they think you're not using them effectively.

When everyone was flying on the company plane from St. Louis to New York, and Otto Graham was asked to go commercial, there was a clear message for him.

When the moment came for everyone in upper management to refurbish their offices and Janet McNeil was told that due to financial constraints, she'd be included in the next round, the message was there for her.

Perks are an important part of the job and of living, and if you sense yours are being eroded, you have every right to worry.

Needless to say, if you're asked to share your office or are given a new office that's smaller or crummier than the first or farther away from the locus of power, you're in trouble. In London one of my friends was once asked to share a "partner's desk" with another person who'd already been exiled to outer Siberia on the grounds that this was the way the British had always done it. Fortunately, he was smart enough to see through that ruse. He eventually left the job. It turned out to be one of the best things that ever happened to him.

10. Someone else is asked to do tasks previously assigned to you. Not a problem if those tasks are minor or unimportant. But if they are activities you especially value, if they are revenue-producing, or if they are an essential part of your job description, you could be in trouble.

As unpleasant as it is to receive negative feedback from your boss, it's better than having him ask someone else to focus on the very project you've been working on. Be alert for this. David

Henderson was producing a series of articles for a pharmaceutical company, and the boss didn't like what he was turning out. So he asked one of David's peers to write the articles. When David approached him about this, the boss simply said, I'd like somebody else to take another crack so I can compare the results.

You won't be surprised to hear that David's material was never used. Once again, the handwriting was on the wall.

What Should You Do?

If one or more of these red flags is waving vigorously in the breeze, you've got to do something. You may be tempted to ask your boss directly, am I in trouble? I would recommend against that. You may or may not get an honest answer. And if perchance you are not in trouble, your question introduces the idea.

Instead, I would say to the boss, we have a problem as a company and I'm here to help you solve it. What can I do to help? If the boss continually pushes back and makes it clear that he doesn't want you to be part of the process, the message is unmistakable. Start looking.

Discontent: the Other Red Flag

Beyond all those external red flags, there's one infallible way to tell if you should be seeking a new challenge: Listen to your gut. If you're bored, if you can't focus, if you're all out of ideas and can't get excited about what you're doing, if you dread going to work, you are psychologically out the door. And don't think that no one notices.

There are many reasons for this kind of inner discontent. Your job may be too limited. Or maybe you've simply done the same thing for too long. Sure, you're good at it, and you could continue to do it for another ten or fifteen years. But you have energy, abilities, and interests that you're not using, and you'd like to find a way to express them.

Or maybe the job itself is satisfying but the environment is not. Either way, it's time to reposition yourself.

Before You Step Off a Cliff, Read This

Before you quit your job, buy a bed-and-breakfast, or otherwise turn your life upside down, consider the following questions:

Are You Financially Secure?

Making a career change normally takes three to six months, and even under the best of circumstances, it's a stressful process. The last thing you need during that time is to worry about paying the bills. Before you take a drastic step, figure out your monthly debts and expenses and multiply by six. If you've got that much money stashed away, great. You can devote yourself to the process of creating change with 100 percent attention.

If you're short of funds, you need to proceed with caution. If you're unemployed, you might want to take a part-time job while you're looking for something more permanent. Otherwise, the financial anxiety you're likely to feel will warp the process, and you may end up jumping at the first job you're offered, whether it's right for you or not.

Are Your Family and Friends Behind You?

Once it becomes known that you're looking for something new, you want to surround yourself with people who will cheer you on. Equally important, you want to avoid people who aren't supportive—and there may be more of them than you expect. Among those killjoys could be your parents, who were probably raised in the Depression and may never have recovered; a few so-called friends and colleagues who will condescend, making you feel even worse; one or two people who will take pleasure in the thought that you fumbled the ball in some way; and the occasional jerk who will wonder, to your face or to your back, whether you've lost your edge.

Most dangerous of all, there are those who will appear to commiserate and yet will somehow manage to project all their own anxieties on you. It's tough, they'll say, for someone in your field. No one wants to hire anyone over fifty. You're the wrong gender. You're the wrong color. The economy is a wreck. You don't stand a chance.

Who needs that? Stay away from those nay-sayers and pessimists if you can. If you're lucky, your family and close friends will be supportive. If they're not, contact the people you know who have made similar changes; try to forge a connection with younger friends and colleagues, who may be less intimidated by the implications of change; or step up to the plate and seek advice from a therapist or job counselor. Better to pay for support than not to have it at all.

Do You Have a Direction?

Change for its own sake is pointless. You need to know where you're heading. But the reality is that early in the game, you may feel at sea. Here's how to determine your direction.

Determining Direction

You can determine a general direction, if not a specific goal, through three simple steps—but only if you are completely honest with yourself.

Identify Your Guiding Principle

What one or two aspects of work mean the most to you? It could be money, travel, power, security, creativity, independence, exercising leadership, and so on. These big concepts are the first elements you want to identify because if your work life lacks them, it doesn't matter what else it may have, you won't feel content.

Name Your Preferences

Focus on some smaller concerns by answering the following questions: Are you attracted to multi-national corporations with thousands of employees or small, independently run enterprises? Do you like to work alone or in groups? Do you enjoy working in an office or away from an office? And if you prefer an office setting, is it important to have all the trappings or can you work in a cubicle? Are you comfortable in an open, free-wheeling environment where all ideas can be discussed no matter how bizarre—or do you prefer a more structured situation? Do you prefer to work on salary or on commission? Because issues like these can deter-

mine your day-to-day happiness, it's important to decide what really matters to you and what you can give up if you must.

For instance, many corporations have rules about how you dec-
orate your office. Some companies will only allow employees to
hang a single picture on their wall. That kind of rigidity bothers
almost everyone, a least a little. But many people are willing to accept the corporate controls because they appreciate other aspects
of the job, including the security they feel working for an established corporation.

Other people have zero tolerance for regulations like that. They
value self-expression more than they value security and they're
not willing to compromise.

Only you know which group you fall into.

List the Industries You Find Appealing

Do you like education? Health care? The defense industry?
Finance? Non-profits? What about travel and leisure, restaurants,
fashion, or real estate? Are you interested in antiques, wine, or
books? Do you have a secret desire to go into politics?

If you're lucky, the industry you're in is the industry that most
interests you. But maybe you're bored with that world. Perhaps
you took a wrong step twenty or thirty years ago, and now you find
yourself marooned on an island you never really wanted to visit in
the first place. Well, just because you've worked in pharmaceuticals or banking or insurance for most of your life doesn't mean
you're stuck there forever. Plan your escape by making a list of the
industries that appeal to you—and do it with a spirit of optimism
and possibility. This exercise may sound hokey. I have found it to
be remarkably revealing and effective, for it encourages you to
imagine. And imagination is the precursor to change.

But is this exercise useful? Is it realistic to think that a person
over fifty might change industries? The answer is it's realistic only
if you're passionate about it—and if you prepare. That means
gaining a thorough knowledge of the industry you want to get
into; establishing a set of contacts within that industry; and finding a way to communicate within that industry that will distinguish you from others who are also trying to get in the door. It
may also mean making a lateral move, taking a job that's a step or

two below what you're doing now, or establishing yourself as a free agent. Is it worth it? If you care about the quality of life for the rest of your days, it is.

A Multitude of Jobs

There came a time in my own life when I knew I had to leave Hill & Knowlton, the public relations firm where I'd been working for twenty years, and strike out on my own. I needed a clean break. Unfortunately, I wasn't sure what I wanted to do.

So I started to fantasize. I thought, I could be a scriptwriter— and there I was, in my imagination, wheeling down Sunset Strip in a convertible, ready to take a meeting. I could work in a foreign embassy—and I saw myself dressed to the nines at the Court of Saint James, sipping a cordial after a state dinner. I could be a teacher, underpaid but gratified by the work I was doing. I pictured myself lecturing a group of students who would follow me with their eyes, rapt at my every word. In my fantasies, each of these occupations offered major satisfactions. But when I considered the pros and cons of those jobs, I grew indecisive.

Fortunately, someone helped me out of my muddle: none other than Gerry Roche, the Senior Chairman of the Board of the search firm Heidrick & Struggles International, Inc. He's a high-level headhunter who is so well respected that his colleagues voted him "Headhunter of the Century." Lucky for me, he's a friend.

Gerry and I went to breakfast one morning at the Sky Club. I sat at one end of the table and Gerry sat at the other. Then he opened his briefcase and began pulling out job descriptions for searches he was conducting. He must have had forty or fifty job descriptions, and he forced me to consider each one as if it were being offered to me. Did I want to be a salesman? A banker? An airline executive? How about a social worker or a veterinarian? Gerry ran through a long series of possibilities. In the process, he helped me realize what I should have known instinctively—that I love public relations and wanted to stay in that business. Only this time, I wanted to be my own boss.

Everybody can't have Gerry Roche for a friend. But everybody can perform the same kind of exercise that Gerry put me through.

I highly recommend it. You can do this exercise by checking out the jobs listed in professional journals, in the want ads, and on the internet. I'm not talking about a job search here. Far from it. I'm talking about an exercise in the imagination. It can make you appreciate the benefits of the field you are already in, and at the same time, open your eyes to fields that you might not normally have considered.

If You've Been Fired . . .

If that's your situation—or if you suspect that it easily could be—you probably feel intensely discouraged. I would urge you to fight that feeling. So would Gerry Roche. As a preeminent headhunter, he's worked with the best and the brightest, more than a few of whom have been given the boot at some point in their career. Here are his suggestions about how to deal with being fired. You will notice that retiring is not one of them!

GERRY ROCHE

RD: *I know several people who have lost their jobs. I wonder if you ever deal with people in that situation.*

GR: All the time. That's when people come to me. I just finished talking with a guy who was chairman of a ten billion dollar company who lost his job.

RD: *Why do successful people like that lose their jobs?*

GR: In some cases, it's the economy. In some cases, the board decides that they aren't satisfied with the results. In some cases they get into personal difficulties. The reasons are all over the place.

RD: *How do they react?*

GR: The people I'm dealing with have been winners all their lives. They've always been promoted, they've never had to look for a job, and it comes as a psychological shock to them. But these are not people who go off in a psychological funk, feel-

ing sorry for themselves. They have strong personal charac-
teristics—that's how they've gotten to where they are—and
they are not weak. They've handled problems all their lives
and they just look at this as another problem.

RD: *So what do they do?*

GR: Most of them work out a plan: Okay, I'll take three months
off and go fishing and clean up my garage and spend time
with my family and that'll allow me to focus on what to do
next. And then I'm going to talk to Roche and I'm going to
talk to my investment bankers and I'm going to network the
private equity people and I'm going to work a plan. As time
goes by, I should develop some options. Then I'll pick one
and go on from there. That's their attitude.

RD: *Does it make a difference if they're over fifty?*

GR: Despite what you might read, there are plenty of opportunities for people in their fifties and sixties. And it isn't because
of some altruistic do-gooder attitude. It's because these are
experienced, mature people who, assuming they can stand
up to the stress of the job, are a good economic buy for the
potential client.

RD: *Why don't they retire?*

GR: They don't want to. Besides, the idea of saying somebody hits
sixty and automatically has to retire is long since gone. I
mean, Alan Greenspan is seventy-four. Peter Drucker is in his
nineties. I can tell you that Jack Welch at sixty-five has given a
lot of thought to what he wants to do with the rest of his
life—and playing golf all day isn't it.

You know, you don't take thoroughbred horses who have
been running the track every day of their lives and just because a birthday rolls around take them off the track and put
them in a stall and feed them hay. You can't do that. You give
them another track to run. The track might be in a different
city, it might have a different surface, it might have a differ-

ent temperature, but they have to run. Good people don't retire. They have to find another vent for their energies.

RD: *Like what?*

GR: Often they look to non-profits.

RD: *Do they start new careers in the business world?*

GR: To be honest, it can happen, but it's rare. There are so many people, Bob, so many people who come to me with their life's goals and ambitions and dreams unfulfilled, and it's a matter of compromising. People need to be realistic.

On the other hand, to quote Oliver Wendell Holmes, "No generality is worth a damn, including this one." The point being, you can't generalize on age, you can't generalize on function, you can't generalize on industry. That said, there's one generalization I will make: The resilient, the flexible, and the hard-driving, energetic, creative communicators who have good personal skills will do fine at any age.

Gerry Roche has helped thousands of people renew their careers and he knows what he's talking about. Resilience and flexibility are essential. Two other traits are also vital: enough courage to take off in an unexpected direction and enough realism to distinguish between an ambition worth pursuing and a pipe dream. Ask yourself, are the skills I have transferable to this new field? Is there a way I can improve my skills? Will circumstances allow me to make a transition? Most important, do I have the ability? A lot of people con themselves. I've seen it happen repeatedly.

Strangely enough, a huge percentage of these dreamers share a single vision. I hope this doesn't strike you as hypocritical, but I need to issue a warning about one line of work in particular.

Want to Be a Writer?

I once had an employee I'll call Laurie. She wanted desperately to be a writer. But she didn't know what a complete sentence was. She split infinitives all the time, she didn't understand parallel construction or subject-verb agreement, she had no feeling for language, and she lacked imagination. I tried to push her in other directions. Laurie, I'd say, there are things you can do better than writing. And she'd insist, no, I'm a writer. To prove her commitment, she carried around books by Ernest Hemingway. I'd see her hunched over her desk at lunch reading *The Snows of Kilimanjaro* or *A Moveable Feast,* and I would think, this very nice person doesn't have a clue who she is. I tried to move her into research but she couldn't come to grips with it. Eventually I had to let her go.

I tell this story only because the fantasy of becoming a writer seems to be ubiquitous. I meet people all the time who tell me they want to write. My view is this: Unless you have a publisher's contract in hand, do not quit your day job to write a book. Don't even think about it. If you really want to write, see if you can wrest thirty to sixty uninterrupted minutes out of every day. Then close your door, turn on the answering machine, and write. Do this for several weeks. If you find that for one reason or another it's too hard—and it *is* hard, I can assure you—find something else.

Remember that while a book might theoretically become a bestseller and make you a fortune (not to mention a household name), it is far more likely to earn virtually nothing, assuming you're lucky enough in the first place to find a publisher. You have to do it for the love of it—not the money.

Consider, too, the words of Russell Baker. "Writing a book is not a lark . . . ," he writes. "It means sitting alone in a darkened apartment room for two or three years exploring the dimmest recesses of your brain." If that doesn't sound good to you, move on.

What to Want

There's a scene in the movie *Save the Tiger* in which Jack Lemmon and Jack Gilford are talking about their Seventh Avenue rag business, which they are desperately trying to keep alive. At one point Gilford says to Lemmon, who is falling apart, "What do you want? What do you really want?" And Lemmon looks at him and says, "One more season."

I can understand that. Like Lemmon's character, most of us want to stay in the game. Ben Bradlee, delivering the eulogy for Katherine Graham of the *Washington Post,* said that one of the qualities that distinguished her was that she always wanted a piece of the action. I think that's what life is about. Everybody wants to be part of something. Everybody wants to make something happen. Everybody wants magic.

By magic, I'm talking about the camaraderie and stimulation that come from being part of a group that is working on an important endeavor.

I'm talking about the synergy that results when the chemistry is right. I've seen it happen time and again. I've seen it at PepsiCo. I've seen it at Quaker Oats, where Bob Stewart brought together seven or eight young executives who worked together, did wonderful things for the company, and had a great time along the way.

And I'm talking about one other thing: a sense of expansiveness and excitement and possibility. A sense that you're on the cusp of change, that your life is about to take a turn for the better, and that through your own actions, you can make it happen.

That's what I mean by magic.

5

Get a Job

I recently saw an advertisement for one of those internet job sites plastered across the side of a bus shelter. The copy consisted of four words: "Job good. Life good."

My sentiments exactly. Life's too short to spend eight hours a day (or more) doing something that fails to satisfy. No matter how old you are, it's not too late to find a job that's both fun and fulfilling, especially if you live in the United States. Although Europeans talk about reaching economic parity with the United States, in terms of employment they're nowhere close. We have a tremendous economic engine and a robust job machine, and all you have to do is figure out how to make it work to your advantage. What that means, however, depends upon the era.

When I started out in business in the 1960s, successful employment meant cradle to grave. You started on the job and stayed there as long as you possibly could. My father did that and I followed his lead for twenty-five years.

In the 1990s, that ethos disappeared. In a time of great prosperity, everybody was jumping from job to job. The idea was to advance as fast as you could, constantly upgrading yourself in terms of both responsibilities and salary.

That began to change in 2001. Even before the events of September 11, the economy was on a downward slide. In the reordered and recalibrated economy that we've been dealing with since that awful day, most people are staying exactly where they are. There simply aren't as many opportunities as there were during the 1990s.

But I don't think that the notion of staying with one company for life, the way my dad did, will ever return. The 1950s are gone forever. So are the 1990s. We're in an entirely new place. Call it terra incognita.

Part I: Don't Quit Your Present Job . . . Unless You Have To

I once knew a man I'll call Tim. He was an accomplished guy, but for reasons I never understood he was bitter about what he did and he drank too much and it was a bad life. One morning, after a frustrating series of events, Tim walked into his boss' office, slammed the dictionary on the desk, and announced, "I quit."

The boss looked up and said, "Thanks very much, Tim, for coming in and I appreciate your returning the dictionary."

Mollified, Tim said, "Well, I don't really quit."

His boss wouldn't let him back down. He said, "Yeah, Tim, you really have. And good luck."

I don't know what happened to Tim. (I think he may have become a gardener.) I can tell you this: he never returned to the big time.

Even if you despise your job, you don't want to quit rashly (or be fired), and I think everyone understands why: It's easier to get a job if you've already got one. If you're employed, you've passed a test. Potential employers assume that you're okay. If you don't have a job, employers start to worry. Did you do something wrong? Surely you must have . . . in which case, how can they find out what it was? You can circumvent that whole line of reasoning by holding on to the job you've already got, no matter how miserable it may be.

And yet, that puts an extraordinary burden on you. If you're a serious person, you can't help thinking, I've got responsibilities on my current job and I can't take time off to look for another one. Balancing your loyalty to your current employer with your need to investigate other possibilities is not easy. At best, it is an awkward process that involves subterfuge, "personal business" days, late nights with the laptop, and more than the usual amount of anxiety. If you've got a job, that's the way it is.

How to Quit Your Job

If you are absolutely certain you're about to get fired and you'd rather not have to explain that to people, go ahead and quit. Here's how: Tell your boss that you want to depart and that you'd like to say wonderful things about this organization. Tell him that despite everything, you don't have a bad feeling about the company (even if you're actively hoping that Microsoft will squash it like a bug). Tell him that you'd like to have the opportunity to resign for the same benefits you would get if you were fired. If your boss is even slightly humane, he'll go along with your request and you'll be able to say that you resigned.

On the other hand, maybe you'd rather be fired, but your boss—who clearly dislikes you—doesn't want to do it because it will cost the company money. He figures that if he makes you angry enough, you'll quit just to salvage your pride and remove the irritation. I'm reminded of a newspaper executive in Chicago who was brought in to be fired by the big boss. The boss started delivering a series of points, almost all extremely negative, about how miserably this executive had failed. My friend sat there calmly, knowing that if he was fired, he would get two years of benefits. Even when the harshest insult was hurled at him, he just smiled benignly, which only engendered further insults. At the end of the day, however, he ended up with several years of compensation that he would not have received otherwise.

In the end, there's not a lot of difference between being fired and beating them to it by quitting. More people than you might guess, including some very successful men and women, have lost their jobs the hard way.

And remember: No matter how you lost your last job, whether you walked away or were thrown overboard, it's a mistake to say you're out of work—under any circumstances.

Unemployed? Never!

The first thing you should do if you're out of a job is to form your own company. Before you incorporate, choose a creative name (check the internet to make sure that no one else got there first—and don't name your company after yourself unless you fully intend to stay in business). Get some stationery and cards printed up. And talk about your business to everyone. You may find that, once launched, it arouses your interest so thoroughly that ultimately it becomes your business for real. (See Chapter 6 for more on this topic.)

A good friend of mind, a consultant, followed this advice. After he was fired, he immediately went to three friends, all of whom owned small companies, and got them to sign up as clients for a dollar a year—at least in the beginning. One day after he was fired, he was able to say that he had three clients. That led to other clients and ultimately to a very successful business.

It's also possible that you will hate being your own boss. That's okay too because you can still create a home office, deduct business expenses, choose your own hours, and so forth. You have the freedom to hunt for a job you'll love without having to say you're unemployed. And your résumé will have no suspicious holes in it.

Part II: Looking for a Job

To get the right job, you need to be relentless in your search. Limiting yourself to only one method, such as talking to a head-hunter, is a gigantic blunder. If you're serious about finding a job, you need to pursue all possible sources, from the most mundane to the most arcane. Those methods include the following:

Reading the want ads. It is amazing how few people read the want ads. There are want ads in virtually every local newspaper from the *New York Times* to the tiniest small town weekly. In addition, the *Wall Street Journal* runs ads, and those ads change in the regional editions. There seems to be a misapprehension out there that want ads are fine for entry-level positions, academics, and health care professionals, but otherwise they're useless. That's just plain incorrect.

Many people focus solely on the *Wall Street Journal* and other big papers. That's also a mistake. If I were looking for a job, I would also look at small community papers, and I'm including the shopper's news. I've seen interesting jobs advertising in those papers—jobs that can give you a sense of fulfillment in your community and make you some money in the process.

Remember, too, that the ads change. Looking for a job means reading the ads every day.

Checking out trade associations and professional journals. In many professions, several trade journals might apply to you. You should cast your net as widely as possible and read them all. Many people have found great jobs in unlikely places.

For instance, I knew an executive who wanted a job in the television industry. He kept checking all the traditional places—*Broadcasting & Cable, Electronic Media, Variety,* and more. Then one day he happened to leaf through a university publication. And there, behold, was an ad for someone to run its television station—exactly the sort of position he wanted. His qualifications matched those requested in the ad, and he got the job.

Exploring the Internet. In theory, this should be the way to go. In reality, we're not quite there yet. But you cannot afford to ignore the Internet. Once you take the leap into cyberspace, you will discover excellent guides to job-hunting on the net such as The Riley Guide, résumé writing sites such as JobSmart, and sites that offer career counseling. You'll find general employment sites such as HotJobs.com, Monster.com, and Headhunter.net, and specific job sites such as AccountantJobs.com, editorandpublisher.com, and lawjobs.com. You'll see newsletter bulletin boards with job postings and announcements of openings at company websites. There are even sites such as CareerPath.com that enable you to check out classified ads in dozens of newspapers without dirtying your hands. All these are worth exploring.

Another option is posting your résumé on the Internet. A few years ago, this might have sounded like a crazy idea. It no longer is. It's now possible to post your résumé in such a way that a potential employer can contact you but every nut with a get-rich-quick scheme cannot. However, you need to know what procedures to follow as well as how to craft your résumé for this medium. (Tip: Be sure to pepper it with keywords. That way, it's searchable.)

There are a number of helpful books on how to use the internet to hunt for a job. They include:

- *How to Get Your Dream Job Using the Internet: The Only Book That Takes You Straight to Thousands of Jobs Worldwide!* by Shannon Bounds and Arthur Karl.
- *100 Top Internet Job Sites: Get Wired, Get Hired in Today's New Job Market* by Kristina M. Ackley.
- *Internet Jobs: The Complete Guide to Finding the Hottest Jobs on the Net* by John Kador.
- *Job Searching Online for Dummies* by Pam Dixon.

Keeping up with the business news. Many opportunities can be found not in little boxes in the classified section but between the lines in the financial pages. That's where you can discover which companies are about to expand and increase their capital expenditures. Those firms have to make a public disclosure. When they do, you know they're going to hire people with all kinds of experience. Sooner or later, they're bound to place an ad. But why wait until then to apply? Might as well approach them now, before they're deluged with résumés.

Don't eliminate a company because you have no particular expertise in that field. You don't have to be a petroleum engineer to work for Exxon Mobil or a research scientist to work for Eli Lilly. Every company needs financial officers, accountants, personnel people, and so on. Every company needs employees with conventional, flexible skills.

It's also helpful to be aware of industries that are gearing up to expand. Look at it this way: in 1900, there were maybe three or four automobile companies. Now there are about two thousand.

And, despite the dot.com disasters of recent years, we are once again in an expansionary period. In the years to come, high tech industries will become more important, not less. The same is true for stem cell research and other applications of microbiology. Those companies are likely to be hiring. And I can assure you, you don't have to be Craig Venter to get a job in the human genome business.

Seeing a headhunter. Working with a search firm can provide a safety net. It can also be a revealing experience because head-hunters have worked with legions of job seekers. They know what employers are looking for and what qualities drive them away. If you can find a recruiter who will take an interest in you, that's a smart move to make.

On the other hand, using a headhunter is not always appropriate or even helpful. For a detailed discussion of the pros and cons of various types of headhunters, you might want to take a look at John Lucht's book *Rites of Passage at $100,000 to $1 Million+*. And don't let that title intimidate you. It's a useful book even if your income is nowhere near the range he indicates.

Activating your network. Conventional wisdom says that 80 percent of the jobs that you hear about will come directly from people you know. I would not be surprised if the actual number turned out to be even higher.

Recently, for instance, I interviewed a man for a position in my office. He came to us because he knew somebody. Now, this guy is not as uniquely qualified as he probably thinks. Au contraire. There's a tremendous pool of people exactly like him. But since he knew somebody we knew, we were confident that his integrity and abilities were up to snuff, and therefore we're going to take a chance on him. His networking paid off.

Networking means more than handing your business card out to everyone you meet. Asking your contacts to let you know if they hear of something is not enough. You've got to involve them. You've got to get them to be active on your behalf. And you've got to push them to follow through.

Let me tell you: People will be agreeable and responsive when you talk to them. Everyone will promise to help. But will they? No.

Most people, most of the time, will never get around to it. So you have to follow up. How do you do that? In my experience, it comes down to incessant phone calls.

Work Your Network

Here are a few ways the people in your network can assist you:

- Ask for their advice. There's undoubtedly something you haven't thought of that the people in your network can provide. Individually and collectively, they have knowledge that you need. Make it easy for them to give it to you.
- Ask for strategic help. This is especially useful when you've got a vision but not a plan. You can say to the people in your network, I know what I want to do. Can you help me figure out how to do it?

  I recently ate lunch with a prominent fellow who doesn't need a job but wants a position in the government. He called on me, as part of his network, to help him figure out some strategies he might use. You should do the same with the people in your network.

  No matter what your line of work, you know people who know how to strategize. They may not be in the business of giving advice. But take my word for it, they'll be glad to oblige.
- Ask for a reference. Assuming you choose wisely, most people you approach will say yes. Follow up by asking what they would say about you. That forces them to think about your strengths and articulate them, a process that provides you with useful information and underlines in their minds what a terrific human being you are.
- Ask for help getting into a specific company. If you know anyone who works with the company in any capacity—as an executive, as a supplier, as a salesman, or even as a journalist who reports on that industry—you can ask that person to recommend you to someone in the company. That's a time-honored way to get in the door.

- Ask for job leads. It's not easy to do that, but in an economy like this one, you have to be forward.
- And finally, be forthright and ask for a job. Most of the time, you will be told that it's too bad you weren't around a few months ago because, unfortunately, they're not hiring now. But if you do it right, if you present yourself in the right way, you can tilt the odds in your favor. Stay with me, and I'll tell you how.

Part III: Applying for a Job . . . Even if There Is No Job

Let's assume you've found a position that interests you. You might have seen it advertised in the want ads or on the internet. More likely, a friend or acquaintance called you out of the blue (after weeks and weeks of nonstop networking) and told you that Company XYZ was looking for someone with your skills.

The first thing you want to do is to send a letter that will distinguish you from the rest of the pack. That means making sure you're dealing with the right person. Rarely will that be anyone in personnel, because the people in personnel, able as they are, just act as a filter, weeding out some candidates and recommending others to somebody at a higher level. You're better off if you can figure out who that higher-up is and start there. If you're not sure, go directly to the CEO.

And be certain to find out something about that person. This used to be difficult. Thanks to the Internet, it no longer is. You might say, I know that Company XYZ is hiring, and since you graduated from Ohio State . . . or since you live in my home town . . . or since you share my interest in international politics . . . I thought I'd write to you. You have to throw in something extra, a mickey to get their attention.

Other points to address in the cover letter:

- Instead of talking about what a peerless candidate you are, establish your interest in the company. I would write the CEO and say, I've thought a lot about your company, I've admired it for years, and the job you've done is terrific. Be specific enough to prove that you know what you're talking about.

• Summarize what you bring to the table. You might say something like this: Not only will I bring enthusiasm and experience, I'll bring a knowledge of your industry and of the way you operate. I'll be able to get you one plus one equals seven or eight. That's why I want to come to see you. You may not have the time to see me, but if you refer me to the right person, I'll knock the socks off the ball for you.

Or words to that effect.

Note that you can write a letter like that even if the company has not advertised a job opening. And remember: the letter is just part of your job-seeking package. In addition, you're going to include a résumé—and much, much more.

Writing Your Résumé

The average résumé is written for file 13. It's generally a stilted piece of prose filled with bureaucratic doublespeak that nobody cares about or even reads.

It doesn't have to be that way. The purpose of the résumé is not to present a series of factoids about who you are and what you did. The purpose of the résumé is to surprise the person on the other side of the table in a positive and elegant way.

To craft an effective résumé, keep these five points in mind:

1. Provide results. Don't just say you've done something. Say it produced results, and be as specific as possible. People were motivated, productivity rose, circulation increased, accidents declined, new products were invented, and so on. Talk about the result, and if you can back up your claim with numbers, do. "Sales increased" is good. Sales increased by 62 percent is better.

2. Prove your point. Most people state that they're in excellent health on a résumé. Not enough. Add that you're a runner or a

kayaker or a mountain climber. That detail illustrates good health, suggests that you're a high-energy person, and implies that you've got a life—not just a suit.

3. Customize the résumé. This is not the moment for one-size-fits-all. If you want a job with Boeing, say so. And use the word Boeing throughout the résumé. With modern technology, it's easy to do that.

4. Do something that makes the person want to read the résumé. Picture your would-be boss sitting at a desk overflowing with résumés. To get her to pick your résumé out of the pile, you've got to distinguish it in an interesting, dignified way.

If I wanted a job with Texaco, for instance, I would go on line and print out all the news stories about Texaco over the last two months. Then I'd put them in an attractive binder with my résumé on top. I've learned so much about the company, you can say, and I'm including the research to demonstrate that I'm not just going through the motions.

Your would-be boss will not be able to resist opening the binder.

5. Don't exaggerate. You were technically managing editor but you might as well have been editor-in-chief? Don't even think about it. You worked as a Christmas replacement from December 18, 1992 to January 2, 1993? Do not write "1992–1993" on your résumé. It won't wash.

According to a recent article in the *Wall Street Journal,* 23 percent of executive résumés contain exaggerations—about their accomplishments, about the size of the organization, about the number of years spent on the job, about their pay. Can you get away with it? Maybe. But if you're found out, and you easily could be, it looks very, very bad.

Yet people lie on their résumés all the time. My beloved alma mater, Notre Dame, was embarrassed recently when they hired a coach who, five days into his first season there, turned out to have lied about his degree. His name was splashed across the front page and he was forced to quit. Don't take that chance.

Collateral Materials

No matter how well-organized it might be, a résumé tends to turn even the most engaging personality into a highly accomplished dullard. To keep that from happening, I recommend adding one or two short essays about yourself, your career, and the company you're hoping to work for. Here's what one such essay might include:

Ten Great Points About You

I'm not talking about accomplishments, honors, or job descriptions. I'm talking about personal qualities, like honesty, creativity, determination, and the ability to stay cool under pressure. List ten or so traits that accurately describe you and customize those points to the company. You might, for example, claim the following:

- A high level of integrity. You could add that, in an industry that is constantly challenged for its business practices, integrity can be notable for its absence. I know Company XYZ isn't that kind of company, which is one reason I'd like to work there.
- The ability to be a self-starter. I can work without somebody kicking me in the pants and ordering me to get moving. That's particularly important in this company because I know that you intend to expand over the next five years. You'll need self-starters to make that happen.
- Imagination. This company needs to think about the opportunities and the challenges that it faces. Opportunities coming down the road include new ways to sell through different channels; challenges include an increased level of federal regulations. In both cases, I've got thoughts on how to maximize profits.
- The ability to motivate. I know how to get the best out of other people. I understand that you don't want people working as isolated individuals in your company. You want them working in teams. I know how to make that happen. I know that teamwork is one of the hallmarks of your company. That's why I want to work there.
- A respect for quality. I reject the second-rate. My career has

been spent on quality projects, and I plan to continue that. I can bring a high set of standards to your company that will raise all boats.

What to Say if You're Switching Careers

Your best shot at making that happen is if you have a transferable skill that can be useful in many businesses. For instance, let's say you're an accountant or a writer. You want to continue working in that capacity but with a different focus. Before you even think about applying for a job in the industry that appeals to you, I would sit down and write 1,000 words on why I've decided to leave insurance for defense; why I've chosen to become a medical writer rather than an art writer; why I've resolved to leave private enterprise for the public sector. Within those 1,000 words, be sure to discuss at least four or five reasons for making the shift. Include that short essay with your résumé. Then, you can say to the people you talk to, I thought about this carefully and I documented my reasons for doing it.

If you have trouble coming up with several solid reasons for changing careers, it may be that you've been fooling yourself. The new field may not be right for you at all, and in your heart you know it.

All of us have wanted to do things in our lives that are probably beyond our capabilities. When I was young, I longed to be a professional football player. The truth is, my reflexes aren't what they should be. At this point in my life, I'm glad I didn't do it. I've had an absorbing career in public relations—and I've still got most of my teeth.

But if you've got a dream that is nagging at you, there's no reason not to pursue it. Writing this essay will clarify your reasons for making a shift and strengthen your résumé by answering the inevitable question: Why are you doing this?

Hot Tip No. 1

Putting a résumé package together is a challenge, and it often takes longer than you expect. So when you finally complete it, your impulse may be to run the nearest FedEx and send it off posthaste.

Restrain yourself. You don't want your package to arrive on a Monday. That's when most people are focusing on meetings, goals, and their personal agendas. No one wants to look at a stranger's résumé.

By Thursday and Friday, the pressure is on. With deadlines looming, people are desperately trying to finish up before the weekend. They'll put your résumé aside and forget about it.

But on Tuesday and Wednesday, people still feel organized and in control. The week is progressing well, they figure they've got plenty of time to do everything, and they're happy to look at a résumé. That's when you want your material to arrive.

If you want to make a strong impression, consider bypassing the Post Office and hand-delivering your résumé. Look your best. Make sure there's an appropriate cover letter written on classy, embossed stationery. And don't forget: Befriend the secretary. (See below for more on this essential topic.)

Hot Tip No. 2

Two or three days after you've sent off your letter and résumé, start a campaign to know the boss' secretary. I would call her on the phone and say, I just sent a note to Mr. Great, and I really want to see him. If he won't see me, I hope you'll refer me to somebody else.

If she brushes you off, as may happen, you should still try to creatively ingratiate yourself with her because an executive secretary usually holds the keys to the kingdom. She is not only the unofficial gatekeeper, but often wields considerable power and influence within the organization because of her closeness to the top man whose time and privacy she zealously protects. There's nothing better than having her say, Mr. Jones has been persistent, he really wants to work here, and I think you ought to see him. That's a third-party endorsement of the most desirable kind.

The novelist Al Irwin, who used to be chairman of the Texas Public Utility Commission, always brought roses when he visited the secretary at a certain firm. The boss never knew that Irwin brought the roses but the secretary did, and it helped him gain immediate access.

Once you've succeeded in getting to the boss, remind yourself to thank the secretary. Send her a note. Send her flowers. Let her know the meeting paid off. Whatever you do, don't ignore her. On the way out of the meeting, Irwin would always stop and kibbutz for a moment with the secretary. And if there was some way he could do something for her, he would extend himself. The efforts he put into his relationship with the secretary paid tremendous dividends.

Hot Tip No. 3

If you have the money, buy a share of stock in the company before the interview. Then you're able to say, I'm a shareholder and I have confidence in the company.

More importantly, owning a share of stock gives you access to all company documents, special leverage when it comes to writing the corporate secretary, admittance to annual meetings, and more. One company that takes full advantage of all this is the *Wall Street Journal.* Recognizing the importance of attending annual meetings, the *Journal* has purchased at least one share of stock in every single company listed on the New York Stock Exchange. They send representatives—that is, reporters—to every one of those meetings. They can do that because they own stock. And so can you.

Part IV: The Interview

The way you interact in a job interview makes all the difference. The last thing you want to do is to just sit there. You want to appear engaged, informed, and at ease. That means you have to prepare. And let me tell you right now, that is no easy task.

Do Your Homework

Most people don't do well in interviews. They're either too overwhelmed and anxious to respond appropriately or too taken with themselves to think that the outcome is in any doubt. Either way, they make a poor impression. You've got to decide in advance what you want to say about yourself. You can only make three points at the most, so it's essential to think about what they ought to be. Making that decision is priority number one.

It's also important to make the interviewer feel good. You can do that by learning something about him. In days gone by, you had to go to the public library and hope to find a listing in *Who's Who*. That was before the internet.

These days, anyone who goes into an interview without knowing something about the interviewer's CV is a moron.

You should be able to find out where this individual was born, where he grew up, and where he went to college. You should know who the president of that university is, and how well the sports team is doing.

And you should know what jobs this person has held. Are you applying for a position in marketing? You should know if he ever worked in marketing. Chances are he did, or he wouldn't be interviewing you. Whatever his experience was, you should relate to it in some way.

In the interview, you can deal with this in a light, conversational way. What you're really doing is talking with the person about his favorite subject. At the end of the day, most people want to hear about themselves. Might as well oblige.

A friend of mine named Karen is a master at this game. She always goes to great pains to find out the likes and dislikes of the person she is talking to. She generally starts the conversation by pointing out something she knows the interviewer likes. That sets the tone for the entire meeting. If she learns the interviewer went to Lehigh University, then she learns a few factoids about Lehigh and plays them back to the interviewer. If she learns the interviewer was born in Scranton, Pennsylvania, she finds something about Scranton and asks the interviewer about it. And I might add that she's never had any trouble getting a job.

First Words

If it's true, as experts think, that we form indelible impressions of other people in only a few seconds, the first words you say to a person can shape the entire relationship. In an interview, you want to choose those words with one objective in mind: to get a positive response.

I recommend starting off by saying something like, thank you for seeing me. It's especially good to be here because I've learned so much about you and your company.

Or you might say, Ford is a great company and I've always wanted to work here.

Or you could glance at the photographs around the office and say something like, it must be wonderful to have such a handsome family.

Then stop. Let your interviewer respond. Don't jump in if he doesn't say anything right away. Silence is a powerful tool, and there's no reason to be afraid of it. As one of the great Indian gurus once said, silence is conversation. In this case, your interviewer is going to have to say something positive. That's your goal. You want to get your interviewer to say yes right from the beginning. It's the most basic principle of salesmanship. And it works.

When the interviewer is talking, listen attentively. Then try to ask questions that relate directly to that topic. It makes a huge difference. I know many job seekers who are so anxious to tell their whole story that no one else gets a word in edgewise. Those people generally fail.

On the other hand, I know an executive named Ron who listens better than anybody I've ever met. When it's his turn to speak, he responds with comments and questions that go directly to the other person's remarks. I've interviewed many, many men and women in my life, and I can assure you: surprisingly few people possess this skill. Those who do have a definite advantage.

The Big Cheese

Recognize that while you want to impress, you can't appear to be more important than your interviewer. That person, at least in the context of the interview, is the master of your fate. You want to allow that person to luxuriate in the feeling of power and competence, and at the same time to enjoy talking with you. So you don't want to dominate. Nor do you want to sit there passively, forcing your interviewer to do all the work. Ultimately, you want the interviewer to feel good about you—and great about himself.

Stay on Point

Research tells us that in most conversations, people tend to remember between 15 percent and 25 percent of what's said. They forget the rest. So if you're going to make a point, you have to make it repeatedly and in a variety of ways. Otherwise it won't be recalled.

Let's say you want to be remembered as a person who is committed to quality in the workplace.

You might begin by saying, I've seen quality throughout your company. I've seen it here, I've seen it there. I'm impressed because quality counts for me too. I can bring quality to the company this way and that way and another way.

By now, you've made five or six points about quality, and you have delivered your message. Although your interviewer will not recall the fine details of what you said, he will remember that quality was important to you and that you thought his company reflected it. When he tells his colleagues about you, he's going to say, this one person couldn't get off the theme of quality no matter how hard I tried to get past him. I think it's something we should think about.

Answers to Questions You Don't Want to Get

Explaining the Gap

If there is a gap in your job history, you can be sure your would-be boss will ask you about it. Better be ready with a good explanation.

This used to be a problem for women who quit their jobs to have children. In the 1980s and 1990s, women who returned to the marketplace were frequently offered menial jobs on the theory that they'd taken too many years off and were behind the curve. That doesn't happen as much anymore. Most employers recognize the importance of taking off time to raise children.

They do not recognize the necessity of dropping out, vegging out, or acting like a member of the leisure class. If you've spent too much time doing too little, you've got to reframe the experience. You could say—assuming there's a germ of truth in it—that you were writing a book but ultimately weren't pleased with the results and decided to return to work. You could say that you made the decision to devote yourself to family during a rough period. You could say that you sailed around the world on a tramp steamer—assuming you actually did do that—because you wanted to get a hands-on sense of our global society.

In short, no matter what you did, it was constructive and even admirable.

I once worked with a woman who took more than a decade out of her career to raise her family. When she finally decided to return to the workplace, she took pains to point out that she had kept up with her industry and done a great deal of writing to prepare herself for her return. In other words, she addressed the gap positively, presenting the missing years as a period of accomplishment. That's the way to do it.

Fired for Cause?

You don't want to lie about it. Lying is counter-productive. But nor do you want to admit that you were single-handedly responsible for putting your company into the red. What should you do?

Say that you separated from this organization. It was right for them, it was right for you, and it was better that you took your benefits the way you took them. If the separation wasn't amicable, and of course it wasn't, you can say that if you must. But don't get stuck on that point. You're better off taking the high road. You bear them no ill will. On the contrary: By and large, your time there was remarkably gratifying.

Afterwards, you can say, you decided to devote yourself to something you'd always been curious about: becoming a consultant, a freelancer, or an entrepreneur. You're glad to have had that experience. However, you soon realized that you'd rather collaborate with other people . . . or work in a corporate environment . . . or pour your energy into an established non-profit. You can say, I've learned that interaction with other people stimulates my creative juices. My best ideas come when I'm able to platform off what other people do. I like teamwork. That's why I'm here.

Last Words

Always end your interview with a question that cannot be answered with a no. You might ask, What makes sense to you in terms of getting this done? or, How do we accomplish this? How can I help take this forward? The knee-jerk response will be, we'll think about that. Or, we can do that at another time.

Your response should be, I'm here right now, and I can help you now. Won't you give me an opportunity?

It's hard to say no to that. Once you have a response, you have a basis on which to make future contact.

I understand that advice like this makes people uncomfortable. No one wants to be aggressive. But in a climate like this one, being pushy underlines your enthusiasm for the job and keeps you in the game.

Dealing With Age

I'd be lying if I said that age wasn't a factor. It is, especially in certain fields. For instance, if you live on the West Coast, it's difficult to tap into the film industry if you're over forty or even over thirty. On the East Coast, you stand a better chance of overcoming that bias.

Television has a similar pattern. On the left coast, you've got to be young to qualify. Here in the original thirteen colonies, age is less of a problem. Just recently, I met with a television group in search of someone to run its programming. They are considering three candidates who are over sixty. They want a seasoned veteran who can motivate young people.

Nonetheless, if you're over fifty, your age is usually not a plus. You don't want to dwell on the issue, but you do have to address it. I would do that by touching upon it lightly and in positive ways. You might say something like the following:

- I've had seventeen years of experience doing this
- I've worked in thirty-eight companies all over the world doing this
- It's taken me fifteen years to learn this

• When I talk to younger people, I find that they know some of what I'm talking about but they don't see the whole picture.

Transitional comments like those allow you to bring the subject up in a way that reflects well on you. You might also say to the interviewer, especially if she's younger than you are, I understand that you're looking for a seasoned and veteran talent, aren't you? That tag question at the end practically forces her to say yes. And once the question has been answered in the affirmative, the door is open.

The Truth About Age Discrimination

Employers will tell you that they want to hire young people because they're bursting with fresh, creative ideas. The real reason, in my view, is that young people cost less. Older people make larger salaries and their health benefits are more costly. Getting rid of them is an economic decision.

Not hiring them in the first place can also be a legal decision. Your potential employer is worried that, if things don't work out, he won't be able to fire you. If he does, you can sue him for age discrimination, tie him up in court, and cost him a lot of money, even if he wins the case. He knows that you're protected by the Equal Employment Opportunity Commission (EEOC), and it doesn't make him happy.

Once you've got the job, the EEOC regulations are indeed a safeguard. But while you're on the market, age discrimination regulations work against you. As one executive told me, off the record, "It's an example of the law of unintended consequences. People over fifty are walking liabilities. That's not to say that we don't hire people who are over fifty. We do. But it's an obstacle."

How can you ease his pain?

• Be flexible in your salary requests. If you can demonstrate that you'll take a job for less than a younger person, you increase your chances of being hired. (It helps that many young people vastly overestimate their skills and are unbelievably greedy.) True, it means compromising your pride. If the job is sufficiently exciting, accepting a lower rate of pay is a small sacrifice.

- Don't demand a contract. Naturally, you'd prefer to get one. But demanding a contract can keep you from landing the job, and you don't really need it. Once you've got the job, your age protects you.
- Show your willingness to work in a less than conventional way, perhaps as an independent contractor. For more on that topic, see Chapter 6.
- Let the interviewer know you're not desperate. Tell him, I'm committed to making this work but if it doesn't, I have other options and it's easy for me to take one of them. You don't want to lie, but I think that's an important thing to say.

Part V: The Campaign Begins

Many people think that once you've sent out your résumé and had your interview, the application process is over. In fact, it has only just begun. Follow-up is everything. Most people don't do it.

Tactic No. 1

After the interview, have the courtesy to write a thank you letter. Nobody does that, so you will immediately distinguish yourself from the pack. In the letter, you want to do a number of things:

- Thank your interviewer for seeing you
- Remind her of the points you tried to make
- Say that you're looking forward to hearing from her. And add that if you haven't heard from her by a certain date, you're going to get back to her
- Arouse her curiosity by indicating that you know something she doesn't know

    You can say, There were two or three additional points I wanted to make during the interview but given the time we had together, I didn't get to them. Don't say what those points are. Indicate that you'd like to discuss them with her when you next get together.

Or you might say, I've done additional research. I've spoken to a number of security analysts about your company, or I've had the chance to chat with several of your customers. They've got a definite view and I thought you might be interested in hearing it.

- Ask her to refer you to someone else

    For instance, if you're a stockholder in the company—and you should be for this purpose—you can ask her to refer you to the CFO or the head of industrial relations for more information. Since you're a stockholder, she has to do this, although it's not something she would normally do. By doing it, she becomes invested in you. And once you get in touch with the CFO or anyone else in the company, you can write her back, thank her for the contact, and say you learned something. And that's another reason why you would like to get together.

Tactic No. 2

I've mentioned this before and I'll mention it again. The boss' secretary is a powerful player. Thank her. Send flowers. Use the same kind of techniques you used before, being certain to make the point that you want to help the boss look good. That's where your interests coincide with hers.

Tactic No. 3

The third follow-up involves finding someone to intercede in your behalf. This is where your network comes in handy. Let's say you know a security analyst who works with the company. You say to him, I don't want to compromise you, but I have an idea that might improve the quality of the company's product or increase the price of its stock. I think it's worth considering. Would you be willing to advance my idea and me as the author of the idea?

If the analyst says no, the answer's no. But he might say yes. If that happens, you're one step closer to getting the job.

Is all this a lot of work? You bet. The key lies in not getting discouraged. You cannot permit yourself to languish in feeling bad about yourself.

Besides, as Arnie Previs of *Forbes* magazine has told me, "the sale begins when the first person says no."

The Meaning of Life

It comes down to this: Life is about having a good time, doing interesting things, and making a contribution. If you're over fifty, you want your job to hit all three of those bases. Here's what you don't want:

- You don't want to work for a tyrant.
- You don't want to work for somebody you dislike.
- You don't want to work for somebody who is deceptive, small-minded, or prejudiced.

Don't do those things. Life's too short.

A Vision . . . and a Kick in the Pants

A few years ago, I met an older man at Disneyland who was running one of the trains. I asked him, "Why are you doing this?"

"Oh," he said, "it's fantastic. I've got the air in my face, I'm talking with young people, I get all the junk food I want, and I'm having a fantastic time. It's much better than my old job at Lockheed Martin, where I was stuck behind a desk with all my pens in a plastic holder so I didn't get ink on my shirt. I was bored and restless. Compared to this, it was terrible."

When we reached the station, I watched as he jumped off the train to help the kids. He had a smile on his face that I am certain he never had when he was wearing that pocket protector at Lockheed Martin. He was clearly a happy man.

That's what it's all about.

You don't have to work at Disneyland to have that experience. You can have that kind of experience in dozens of high-level ways. But it takes effort . . . a lot of effort.

I talked about this with headhunter Hobson Brown, Jr., President and Chief Executive Officer of Russell Reynolds Associates, an executive search firm. I asked him what quality distinguished those people who successfully found new jobs from those who didn't. Here's what he said:

> I find that those people who get themselves repositioned soonest tend to work harder at this than anything they've ever done in their lives. Getting a job is a full time job. It is a huge task. And because it is a word-of-mouth business, it involves extensive networking. Everything else being equal, the people who work hardest are the ones who do the best at relocating themselves.

I find that strangely reassuring. You can't control the economy or the demand that might exist for your particular skills. But one thing you can control: the effort you put into it.

6

On Your Own

Let me tell you about Ted Feurey. He's an amazing guy who runs his own company, T. V. Feurey, and also works with The Dilenschneider Group as chief communications consultant. He's not on my payroll: I wish he were, but he's too independent for that. So I provide him with some office space and in exchange he does a lot of consultant work for my clients as well as for other corporations.

Earlier in his career, he was all over the news business as a reporter, then a news director, then the general manager of a wire service. In addition to newspapers, he worked for radio and television. He traveled widely, and he even spent a satisfying year, when he was around forty, as an adjunct professor at Columbia University's Graduate School of Journalism. He had the kind of career many people would envy.

Even so, when he got to be around fifty, he grew restless. In his desire to try something he might enjoy more, he decided to combine his love of teaching with his knowledge of journalism. He set up a business as a communications counselor.

That was about twelve years ago. Since then, he's worked with doctors, lawyers, business people, and literally half of the Fortune 500 corporations. He teaches his clients how to develop a message, how to deliver a message, how to anticipate questions, how to respond to questions, how to deal with people who do precisely the sort of thing he used to do as a journalist.

Here's what Ted has to say about going out on your own after age fifty: "You can't go through fifty years of life without having acquired some specialized skills. At some point, you say to yourself, I'm going to put these skills to work for me. I want to be the last son-of-a-bitch I ever work for."

A lot of people, myself included, feel similarly.

If you want to be your own boss, you can either buy an existing enterprise or start your own. Those two possibilities are the subject of this chapter.

Buying a Business

The number of businesses sold in America every day is astounding. Look in the classifieds, and you'll see that every kind of business you can imagine is for sale. There are truck stops and pizza places, bed-and-breakfasts, travel agencies, advertising agencies, real estate offices, entertainment companies, businesses that specialize in masonry, manufacturers, and stores of every stripe.

It's phenomenal what's going on. Buying a business can be easier and less risky than starting one from scratch. But you have to go into it with your eyes wide open. Before you decide to buy, make certain you can answer yes to every one of the following questions.

Question No. 1: Do you know why the business is for sale?

If the proprietors are selling because they're old and want to cash out, that's one thing. If they're selling because they want to create a formula whereby you provide them with an ongoing income stream, that's another. If they're selling because the business is a dog, that's still another. One way or another, you need to figure out their motives.

Occasionally, when people have built up a business over a period of years, they will hire an individual with the intention of selling him the business somewhere down the line. That worked well for two men in their seventies who ran a small printing company in Columbus, Ohio. They had a thriving operation printing brochures, booklets, advertising flyers, and all kinds of other stuff. Because they took great pride in the business, they wanted it to go to someone who could maintain its reputation. They brought a younger man into the company and trained him thoroughly. When they were ready to retire, he took over all the sales and contacts. It's been fulfilling for everyone concerned.

You might think that most proprietors would prefer to sell to someone who's already on staff. In fact, it rarely happens. Many owners fear that, if they were to sell to an employee, they would have to divulge what they've been taking out of the business. In many cases, they've been taking out far more than the employees think. Figuring that the employees would be upset if they knew just exactly how good the profits really were, they decide to sell to a stranger and avoid the discord entirely.

But sometimes owners look for a stranger because the business is in trouble. Naturally, the owners will do their utmost to hide those problems from you. That's why you need to do your research. You need to delve into that business's history and financial status. And you need to reach a complete understanding with the owner—in writing—of exactly what you're buying.

A friend of mine didn't do that. He purchased a flourishing consulting business from an owner who wanted to retire. What my friend didn't learn until it was too late was that the owner kept all the customer contacts. Without those names and numbers, the business was worthless. It was a disaster.

You've also got to realize that in most cases the proprietor is not the only person who feels intimately involved in the business. In addition to employees, suppliers, customers, and so forth, the owner's family may think of themselves as part of the business. That's especially true when the business shares the family name.

In one case, a man who had created a successful brokerage house was dying. He wanted to sell the business to his protégé, who was anxious to buy. The protégé, legal documents in hand, visited his boss on his death bed and literally took his arm and had him scrawl his signature on the dotted line. When the boss' wife came in from another room and discovered what had happened, she was horrified. She didn't want the business sold. She wanted it to remain in the family. Furious, she took the protégé to court. She contended that he had acted inappropriately, forcing her husband to sell the business and illegally taking it away from her.

That was about ten years ago. They've been in litigation ever since.

Question No. 2: Do you know what the business is worth?

I think everyone understands that if you intend to buy a business, you have to know what its assets are. Everything from the mortgage to the inventory needs to be included in those calculations. You need to make sure that there are no bad debts or pending lawsuits, that the building is in good shape, that the industry itself is solid, and so on. You also need to asses the intangibles, such as reputation, brand name, and location. You don't want to pay more for the business than it is worth.

Valuation is the key to pricing. In every industry, there is an established set of norms and standards. What you have to do is get a hold of those standards and norms—you can generally find them on the internet—and then take the business apart bit by bit, client by client, customer by customer. Then you can say, this is what it's worth, this is what I see it pulling in, this is what I want to pay for it. Needless to say, the owner will generally place a higher value on the business than you will.

Once you've negotiated an agreed-upon price, you can arrange the payments in a number of ways. For example, you can tell the owner that you'd like her to stay with you for three to five years. At the end of the time, if revenue is above a certain amount, you'll give her a balloon payment or earn-out. If earnings are less than that amount, she gets proportionally less. The beauty of this plan is that there's an incentive for both of you to work together to grow the business.

Whenever you enter into buying a business, think about your own vision for what you're about to buy. How do you intend to improve it? A friend of mine in the nursing home business was intent on taking care of elderly people. He also decided to bring them television, provide them with recreational opportunities, institute an "at home" service where they could leave the nursing home to visit their loved ones, and more. His concept took a business that was worth several million and made it worth tens of millions.

Question No. 3: Can you work with the staff?

The greatest asset of a business is often its staff. Be sure you'll be able to work with those people because otherwise they may leave. And you'll be the one in trouble. I've watched it happen.

A man in the garment business bought a firm that produced a well-known line of casual clothes. The men and women who put the clothes together, the stitchers, were highly skilled and not easy to replace. Unfortunately for him, they didn't like the new owner. When he inaugurated all kinds of petty rules and regulations, the workers refused to accept them. He was adamant. Finally the disgruntled workers rebelled in the time-honored way: They formed a union. The ILGWU came in to help. The owner couldn't meet their demands. And that was the end of his business.

One of the most important things in working with the staff is listening to what they have to say. Often, these are people who haven't been listened to for years. They've got gripes, many of them petty but some important, and they need a willing ear. It's worth taking the time to hear their point of view and then to report back to them. You can say, I've heard everything you've had to say. We can make nearly all the changes you want but we can't accommodate everything.

A CEO in a small company in Ohio did this. He managed to turn a group of hostile, unfeeling employees toward him simply because he listened.

Question No. 4: Are customer relationships in good shape?

Will the customers stay with you? This is often the biggest test of a business. Many times, it turns out that the customers are neither as loyal nor as numerous as advertised. In other cases, the customers stay with the original owner; when he goes, they do too. That's not a good thing.

When I worked at Hill & Knowlton, I bought smaller agencies all over the world. And this is what I learned: You have to kick the tires. You have to do your due diligence. You may discover that most of the significant clients, the ones they bragged about, are on the verge of leaving. That could be why the business is for sale in the first place.

Client loyalty is especially problematical when the business deals in information or advice and collects its customers by word of mouth. If you're buying a gas station, the regular customers are unlikely to care who owns the place. You have every reason to expect them to stick around. With a medical practice or a consulting business, it's another story. The clients are paying for expertise, and they may well move on when the former owner does.

I have a good friend who owned a tavern in Tennessee. He is a likeable, outgoing guy and when people came to the tavern, they responded to his warmth and ended up treating the tavern as a home away from home. Then he sold his business and moved to Florida. The tavern failed miserably because the person buying it didn't have the same ability to connect with the patrons. They came in a few times, missed the previous owner dramatically, and stopped coming. It was a bad deal for the purchaser.

I once bought a business for a dollar. I said to the owner, I'll give you a dollar and if the clients stay around for three years, I'll pay you millions. If they don't stay around, you get the dollar. What happened was that some of the clients stayed and others didn't. I ended up paying more than one dollar but considerably less than the millions we had originally discussed.

As the Romans said, caveat emptor. Buyer, beware.

Question No. 5: Do you have an exit plan?

I contend that when you buy a business you had better think about how you'll be able to get out of it. At what point would you sell? Would you wait until you were teetering on the brink of homelessness or would you sell at the first sign of a slow-down? Do you plan to sell the business when you reach, say, sixty-five? Or are you open to working longer? If you sold the business, what would you do if the new owner asked you to stay on? Would you be willing to do that for a while, even though it might be painful to see things done in a way that could be counter to your judgment? Or are you hoping that your errant daughter, currently trying to make her way as an actress, will see the light and take over your dry cleaning establishment some day? Better have a plan.

In terms of selling the business, courting buyers is like going on a series of first dates: not fun, but how else are you going to find a match? You have be pleasant, you have to dress your business for sale, and you have to offer something that potential buyers want. You want them to realize that you have a solid work force, a unique product, an unassailable location, an impressive profit margin. If you have those things, you can charge a premium for my business. But ultimately, selling a business is as much of an art as buying one. After all, no matter how hot a prospect the business may seem now, you don't want to be stuck with it forever.

Question No. 6: Do you have a formal business plan?

Without one, you might as well be lost in the woods without a map or a compass. A business plan should do the following:

- present a detailed set of objectives and strategies
- identify your niche
- explain your offering and what makes it unique
- provide a marketing plan
- analyze the competition
- include an explicit financial breakdown with projections for the first several years

Writing up the business plan is not the most glamorous aspect of creating a business, but it is possibly the most central. Don't slight it. Begin by visiting the Small Business Administration at www.sba.gov. They have an extensive website which offers, among other services, a detailed fill-in-the-blank business plan.

Question No. 7: Do you really want to do this?

Men and women who have never worked for themselves often have wild fantasies about what it would be like. It's not just the opportunity to make a lot of money that appeals to them, though that's certainly part of it. It's the freedom. That's the part that people find irresistible, even in its most minor application. I've often heard people say, for instance, that they relish the thought of setting their own hours.

But guess what? If you buy a bar or a restaurant, you have to be there constantly. If you buy a store, you may need to keep it open seven days a week from 9:00 A.M. to 8:00 P.M. (And don't forget: You have to arrive early and stay late to take care of the cash register.) If you run a consulting business, you are always on call. When the business belongs to you, you can expect to put in more time, not less, because every problem is your problem. Back in the days when you worked for a corporation, you didn't need to worry about fixing the Xerox machine or counting up the day's receipts or making sure there was a first aid kit on the premises. Somebody else handled it. Now, if you need stamps, you walk to the post office. (Or maybe you ask your assistant to go—in which case, you sit at the front desk and answer the phone.) Every task, however minor, is your responsibility.

Before you buy a business, be sure that you honestly want to run it—not just own it. Will you enjoy being there? Will the business fulfill you in an ongoing way? Do you have the expertise that you need and, if not, can you acquire it? I recommend projecting two years or three years into the future. What would you like the business to be by then? And do you have a legitimate plan to get there? There's nothing worse than deciding to buy a business and then discovering when you're in the thick of it that you don't know how to run it and—worse—that you don't even want to run it. Before you plunk your money down, make sure you know what you're doing.

Talk to a lot of people, including several who own businesses similar to the one you're eyeing. And spend some time in the business section at a good bookstore. Many books investigate the process of buying a business in detail. One recommendation:

How to Become Successfully Self-Employed, second edition, by Brian R. Smith.

Buying a Franchise

The seeming advantage of buying a franchise is that much of the work is already done. The reality is that you can become very wealthy but you have to work like a dog and your ability to be creative is nonexistent. You can't select new products. You can't promote your business in anything other than the prescribed way. Sometimes you can't even pick the music you play. Your ideas are irrelevant. Personally, I wouldn't do it.

But if you want a turn-key operation, go for it—assuming you've got a location that looks hot. That's the key to franchising.

If you buy a McDonald's but it's wedged between a Wendy's and a Burger King, you can only hope to cannibalize their traffic. If you buy a McDonald's in a demographically appropriate community that hasn't previously had one, you'll clean up. And if you decide to purchase a string of seven or eight fast food franchises, you could become seriously rich.

But whether you buy a KFC or a Kinko's, you will have to deal with low-paid laborers who don't love the job, and you will need to stay on top of them. In addition, you have to live within the strictures of the franchise. You want to open an hour later? Change the color of the uniforms? Add a new item to the menu? Forget it. You're not really working for yourself at all: You've got a boss.

Even at Barnes & Noble, you don't get to choose the books. So if you're looking for independence and creativity, the franchise business is not for you. But if you're willing to work hard and don't mind relinquishing the chance to make a personal mark on your business, you could do quite well.

How I Started My Own Business and Lived to Tell the Tale

I started my own business in 1991. It wasn't easy. After many years in a large organization, being on my own felt like jumping off a cliff without a parachute. My entire life, I'd worked under the aegis of a corporation with all the benefits that that entails. Now I had to rely on my own instincts and abilities, and I was scared. For a long time, I kept a quarter in my pocket in case I had to make a phone call. I rode on subways and buses. I never took taxis; as far as I was concerned, they didn't exist.

I created my business with one other person, my assistant Joan Avagliano. We spent a lot of time grappling with the one question every entrepreneur has to ask: What is special about this business? We came up with four basic points.

First, we decided that one answer might lie in my ability to give CEOs strategic advice about both business and public relations. Most PR people don't consider the business as whole, and they certainly don't look at the business in the larger context of society as a whole. In my view, that's short-sighted. I wanted to provide a socio-political analysis and I also wanted to examine the business plan in detail. If it's strong, we can do PR in a way that supports it. If it's shaky, all the PR in Hollywood isn't going to help.

My ability to blend business acumen with public relations was one unique aspect of what I had to offer.

I also thought we could provide a level of service to top CEOs that they couldn't get elsewhere. During my years at Hill & Knowlton, I dealt with literally hundreds of top executives. I thought that CEOs would see me as a person they could confide in. I could provide a sounding board, give them another point of view, and, if necessary, talk back to them. I was somebody they could trust.

That was a second unique aspect of our business.

A third aspect was personal service. I wasn't going to pass important functions on to somebody else. I vowed that my clients would get my attention. I take their phone calls.

Fourth, I was determined to keep our costs at least 20 percent below everybody else's. Did that mean we wouldn't make a profit? I certainly intended to make a profit, and I didn't mind if it turned out to be slightly lower than other peoples'. I figured that keeping my costs low would attract plenty of business.

I also was determined to avoid the minor mistakes that can sabotage a business. I made a list of those mistakes, and I asked friends to contribute their observations. One friend told me to keep my eye on the money. I decided to sign every single check, no matter how small, so I know exactly where the money's going.

Another friend advised me not to have a lavish office. If the office looks like Versailles, clients might think I was using their money unwisely. So we have a comfortable, work-a-day office.

In establishing my business, I took a lesson from the late J. Peter Grace, who said, "Run scared every day of your life." With that in mind, I worked as hard as I ever have. I still follow his advice: I come to work every morning assuming that my business is starting from scratch and it's up to me to make it go.

Once I was certain what services I wanted to offer, Joan and I considered specific ways to keep costs low, to generate revenue, and most of all, to attract customers. We figured we would have to talk to fifteen or twenty potential customers to get one. So we started making lists and going to see people.

I went to people I knew and presented my case. I said, "I know a lot about business and a lot about public relations, and I would like to become your advisor." To my intense relief, these potential customers said yes, and that launched the business.

Since then, I've worked with many people who were starting their own businesses, and I've learned what worked and what doesn't. I'll tell you this: Creating a successful business involves approximately 12,000 challenges—everything from finding a location and negotiating contracts to choosing a logo. But some challenges are more important than others. Here are the basics:

Starting a Business 101

Starting your own business is not an easy task. You've got to incorporate, you need legal papers, you've got to get seed money, and so on.

Before you can even being to think about the details involved in starting a business, make sure you have a calling—not a mild interest or a passing curiosity or a desire to impress your friends. Operating your own business shouldn't be a casual thought. It's too labor-intensive for that. To do it well, you have to be passionate, eager, and resolved. In addition, you have to . . .

Face the Facts

Most small businesses—about 80 percent of them—fail in the first five years. You should know that going in. When you own a business, whether you purchased it as a thriving concern or started it from the back of your SUV, you have to be prepared to endure more anxiety that you ever felt when you worked for someone else, to suffer more public scrutiny, to work longer hours, to take fewer vacations. As almost every successful entrepreneur discovers, there is an intensity to creating your own business that's difficult to escape.

So you have to want to do this desperately.

You also should assume that you're going to have enemies. Your enemies could be jealous neighbors, former clients, the people who still work at the agency that used to employ you. Don't take their enmity to heart: No matter who you are, there will always be someone who doesn't like you. But as you go about setting up your business, these people will try to discourage you. So you have to think that through. You have to figure out how to neutralize them.

You also have to figure out how to combat the Bill Gates scenario in your mind—the one whereby you come up with a brilliant idea and, bingo, you're the richest human being on the planet. It could happen.

But it probably won't. As I said before, most businesses fail.

Develop a Unique Selling Proposition

I once knew a woman who wanted to create a mail order food business. She was a great cook and she talked about her idea all the time. Trouble was, she couldn't decide what to sell. Mango salsa? Two kinds of chutney? Maybe a good basic tomato sauce?

Needless to say, she never fulfilled her dream because she was missing one of the essential ingredients for any business: A clear idea of what she wanted to sell.

Whether you're selling advice or auto parts, you need to know exactly what you've got to offer. You need to find out how it compares to similar products offered elsewhere, and you need to distinguish it from the rest of the field. What makes your PR agency or your photography studio or your garden supply shop unique? You should be able to spell it out clearly and succinctly.

Test Your Market

You might have invented a perfect product: a single vaccine for all diseases, a Mercedes drive-alike for under $5,000, an anti-aging cream that actually works. You might be a cello player who's the equal of Yo-Yo Ma or a negotiator so superior to all others that you really could bring peace to the Middle East. Yet if you can't find customers, it doesn't matter how extraordinary your product is or how skilled you are. Your business will fail.

That's why you have to find out: Is there a market for what I do? Who is it? How big is it? And how can I reach that market?

Some experts might counsel you to hire a market research firm to conduct a mail survey or a telephone survey. I don't think that's necessary. I would begin by talking to your network, begging them to be honest with you, and listening attentively to their responses. Tell them, here's what I intend to do: I'm opening a restaurant, I'm becoming a consultant in environmental affairs, I'm selling rebuilt antique stoves. What do you think? Is there a market?

If you don't get a positive response, rethink your plan. Most businesses work by word of mouth. If you can't get endorsements from your network, you're unlikely to get them anywhere else.

It's also important to check out whether the service or product you intend to sell is available in your area. Hard as it might be to believe, there may only be room for one fountain pen shop in town.

I would also do some research. Visit the Small Business Administration on line. Study publications like *Fortune, Forbes, Business Week,* and the *Wall Street Journal.* What economic trends are they forecasting? What do they think the new industries will be? And does your business fit in with that? In a time of rapid change, flexibility is a requirement. A dream of opening an upscale hotel may have to be put on hold in an era when everyone is afraid to travel. On the other hand, opening a specialty wine shop at a time when everyone wants to stay home could be quite profitable, especially if the neighborhood doesn't offer anything like it.

Do some demographic research to make sure that the people you're hoping to attract to your business live in the area. Don't forget, too, that people over fifty make up an enormous sector of the population. Any business that caters to them is likely to do well.

Develop a Marketing Plan

Once your business is established, you'll want to do some marketing. The type you choose depends on the kind of business you have.

For instance, the other day I wanted to take my son to play miniature golf. So I looked up miniature golf in the yellow pages and found a small ad for a local facility. It turned out to be exactly what we were looking for. The ad worked.

For many businesses, ads are enough. If you're doing nursery work or construction, take ads. If you're selling equipment, take ads. In fact, if you're selling almost any kind of product, take ads.

But for high end businesses—and I consider PR a high end business—I don't think advertising works. Same with doctors and lawyers. In a business based on relationships, you need to generate word-of-mouth. It's that simple—and that complex.

Generating word-of-mouth requires knowing who your customers are and spending time in their world both professionally and socially. It means networking continually and promoting yourself effectively.

In short, it means doing your own PR, a topic I discuss in detail in Chapter 8.

Expect the Unexpected

Even if you buy a business that's a known money-making machine, you should not expect to waltz in and find that everything works the way it ought to. That never happens. You will hit small glitches and large ones. And I guarantee that no matter how well you've done your homework, you will discover at least one nasty surprise. It happens every time.

Commit Yourself

When I started my business, a man named Murray Weidenbaum, the former head of the Council on Economic Advisors, took me to lunch and gave me some great advice. He said, I want you to do one thing. You must pay attention to your clients. If you don't do that, it doesn't matter how great your services are, they're going to leave you after a while.

To illustrate his point, Murray told me the story of several prominent people who left government and started consulting businesses, only to have those businesses fail because they didn't pay attention to their clients. They weren't committed to the client.

At a more modest level, I know a fellow who left his CEO job and bought a chain of four restaurants in the Southwest. The four restaurants were turning three million dollars a year, so it was a pretty good business, and it should have continued to be a success. But he didn't pay any attention to the business. He assumed that the people who were already running the restaurants would do it. They didn't. His restaurant chain went bankrupt.

The moral is simple: Don't buy the business if you don't want to do the work.

But if you are willing to commit yourself, don't let anything get in your way. Ted Feurey, whom I discussed at the beginning of this chapter, has succeeded in creating his own unique business. He has also helped other people make the transition from disgruntled employee to eager entrepreneur. Here's part of my discussion with him:

TED FEUREY

RD: *How should people who want their own business after fifty begin the process?*

TF: First, you should not assume that you've done all that you can do. In an environment that on the face of it looks slightly more youth-oriented, I think that's the worst thing people over fifty can do.

Second, inventory your strengths. If you're over fifty, one would hope that you've developed a number of strengths. In addition to the obvious skills providing the main force of your career, you may have other strengths that you're not putting to use.

RD: *Such as?*

TF: Well, a lawyer may have great strengths in writing or analysis or a variety of fields that are not strictly law. He may want to get out of the law business and into the consulting business. Or he may decide to use the strengths he's developed under-standing corporations. He may want to find a position with a corporation putting to use the years of experience he's had in law.

The same is true in journalism or accounting. I know one public accountant who helped manage the finances for a number of restaurants. At age fifty-two, he got out of the CPA business and opened a restaurant. He liked food, and he un-derstood the restaurant business, and he became very suc-cessful. He knew that the reason most restaurants go under is poor money management. Well, the one thing he knew how to do was manage money, and so he didn't make those mis-takes. It's the old story: People learn from experience. Smart people learn from other people's experiences. That's what I mean by strengths.

RD: *I've spoken to plenty of people over fifty who long to go off on their own but wonder whether it's wise. What should they do?*

TF: Ask yourself, do you need the alarm clock to get out of bed in the morning? Do you look forward to your job? Once that answer is no longer clear, that's a good time for reassessing your personal inventory and saying, wait a minute, isn't there something else I could be doing that's more fun?

There are many cases of attorneys leaving the straight legal business and going into management or finance. I know a lawyer once who was senior partner in a big maritime law practice and he was interested in antiques. Now he and his wife own a successful antiques business.

Another person I know is a doctor, a radiologist. He really liked photography, as opposed to X-ray photography. So he quit medicine and became a freelance photographer. He was close to fifty. Now he does a lot of medical photography. He works for companies that build expensive medical instruments and because he is an M.D., he understands the needs of hospitals and physicians, the people who are buying the equipment, and he understands what the equipment does. And he is very very good at what he does, and extremely happy at it, even though he could probably make more as a doctor.

Let me tell you another story. I worked with a guy at a major communications corporation. He was the president of a big division of the corporation. I had done some work with other people in the corporation, and he had heard about it. And he called me up and said, "Come on over. Let's spend the morning together. I need some public presentation skills. I'm not very good at it."

Turned out he just needed some confidence, a few new approaches, a couple of tricks, and a sense of being at ease and empowered. I wondered why he had called me. I asked, is your role here about to change?

And he said, "No. I'm going to quit my job and become a teacher." That's exactly what he did. He went back and taught high school, because that's what he always wanted to do.

RD: *Using your public speaking skills, no doubt.*

TF: That's why he came to me—to see if he had the wherewithal. It takes guts to leave the nourishing, swaddling environment of a company and wander out on your own. That's why you have to do a forthright inventory of your skills.

RD: *From time to time do you see people whose dreams aren't achievable?*

TF: I've seen people, God bless them for it, who say I want to give this a shot for a year. I want to open a bookstore, or I want to open a small antiques shop, or I want to open a travel agency. There are lots of things you can do. But if you haven't performed at the Metropolitan Opera by the time you're fifty, it's unlikely that you're going to be able to do that.

And yet, I think the worst mistake that people over fifty make is aiming low.

RD: *What do you mean?*

TF: In doing an inventory of their strengths, they underestimate themselves. Again, let's take my friend the accountant. He's a good cook, understands about food, sets a nice table at home. But he has never worked as a chef. He could have gone out and gotten himself a job as an assistant chef or a grill chef somewhere and gotten paid. Well, that's not what he wanted to be. Instead, he went out and managed to get the money to finance a restaurant. He aimed high.

The problem with most people is they aim low and hit. Aim a little higher. You can always readjust your goals.

RD: *Any other tips?*

TF: Seek out people whose opinions you value and who understand what it is you're going through. And be as honest with yourself as you can. Essentially, what is it you'd love to do? Do you want to drop dead chained to an office desk? Or do you want to try something you always wanted to do? What is it you want to do?

RD: *Do you feel that creating something yourself is generally the best way to go?*

TF: Yes. Use what you've got: A network of people who will help carry the ball for you, the skills you've managed to develop, the interests you've developed, the understanding and perceptions that you've been building for years. And put all that to work for you.

RD: *Follow your bliss, so to speak.*

TF: Yes. People say, am I enjoying going to work every day? Or am I just running out the string here until I get to be sixty-five and can retire? If that is what you're doing and you're happy doing that, fine. But I don't know very many happy people who've retired.

RD: *That's interesting. Happy people don't retire.*

TF: That's right. If what you're working for is your pension, maybe you ought to think about re-orienting your life. And you can do that at any age.

RD: *Thank you very much.*

7

Becoming a Consultant

"In every society," wrote Ralph Waldo Emerson, "some men are born to rule, and some to advise."

I have no doubt which group I'm in. I was born to advise (though my kids might disagree). That's why I'm a consultant.

If you feel similarly, becoming a consultant could be a smart move. It's a logical step for anyone who has developed an area of expertise. Not only does it offer the advantages of being your own boss, it makes things easier for the people who hire you. Because you are operating as an independent contractor, they don't have to deal with withholding tax, medical insurance, or putting you on the payroll. You're a free agent. It's a relief for everyone concerned.

As a consultant, you have to be able to attract clients, solve their problems, and make them look good in the process. You also have to be willing to submerge your own ego in order to make your clients—who think they were born to rule—look good.

If you can do that, you can become very successful. Here are the basics.

Attracting Clients: My Method

Most people don't have a clue about how to attract clients. They make cold calls, send out flyers, carry around binders filled with contact sheets and capabilities presentations. It's a tremendous waste of time. The only way to get a client is to meet that person face to face.

But face to face meetings can be intimidating and many people unconsciously avoid them. I recall a colleague of mine who spent eight weeks developing a brochure, tying up people's time by constantly rewriting and interviewing people and dredging up examples and more. I said to him almost every week, this is interesting, but you really have to go see somebody.

He said, I need to finish the brochure first. I knew it was a crutch, and I repeated, you really need to go see somebody. After eight weeks he completed the penultimate draft of the brochure and he sent it to about thirty people, each of whom had a comment. So he revised it for three more weeks and finally the brochure was ready. He told me, now I'm going to develop a list of people to talk to. That took time. In the end, it took literally fifteen weeks before he saw the first person on his list. And when he finally got to talk to that person, the brochure was dated. He wasted about a quarter of a year trying to get business by using a device that created a comfort zone and demonstrated to other people that he was doing something but generated no action at all. In effect he was retarding the process.

When I'm trying to generate work, I do a lot of research and a lot of thinking, much of which will lead nowhere. Yet this is one step you can't skip.

I begin with a list of about twenty-five companies. I don't choose those companies on the basis of special knowledge or inside sources. I choose them on the basis of information I find in the pages of *Barron's*, which provides ready lists of companies that are doing well and companies that are not. I take some of each.

I also apply two other criteria. I only consider companies in the New York metropolitan area, close to where I live. And I limit the list to companies I like. Industries and corporations that I don't particularly care for don't make the cut.

For each company, I make a list of the top officers, the members of the board, and the head of communications. I write down their names, their titles, and anything else I know about them.

Then I get hold of the financial analyst reports and read them carefully. I spend time on the internet exploring the company website and reading anything I can find about the company. On the basis of that information, I try to assess what's going on in the company. I pay particular attention to any communications issue or other internal roadblocks that might be keeping the company from becoming more profitable.

Then I'm ready to start making contact. If I don't know the people on my list, as is usually the case, I check with my colleagues to see if any of them do. If I'm in luck, I'll find someone who can introduce me.

My hope is that if I play my cards right, a few months down the road, five or six of those companies will become my clients.

Who You Gonna Call?

Making the List

The process of making a list cuts two ways. On the negative side, it provides a comfort level that enables us to think we're doing something. On the positive side, the list provides discipline. It focuses your attention and enables you to act in a structured, organized way so that, as soon as you possibly can, you can throw the list away and make a new one.

To generate your list of companies that might benefit from your services, go to the library, spend time on the internet, network like crazy. Try to avoid making a blue sky list topped with companies like General Electric, Exxon Mobil, and General Motors. This is totally unrealistic. You're better off with companies that are number two in their category: Their upper-level people don't like being runners-up, and unlike the self-satisfied executives at the number one companies, they're open to suggestions.

Once you've collected a few dozen firms, pare down the list to ten or so companies that strike you as the most likely prospects. Don't let the reduced size of this list fool you: It will ultimately fill a loose-leaf binder.

Now for each company, do the following:

1. Name names. Name every person in upper management, every person on the board, every person whom you might reasonably expect to meet. Much of this information is available on the internet. In addition, you should be able to learn a certain amount of personal information about many of those people. Anything you can find out will help you enhance your presentation and will enable you to connect with them more easily.

For example, the head of Public Relations at a major Fortune 500 company happens to be a former librarian. Normally, the Dewey Decimal System is a nonstarter in a conversation. In this case, it can open doors.

2. Investigate the company. Surf the web or go directly to Bloomberg.com, where you can check out the ups and downs of the stock, the comparative returns, the fundamentals, and much more, including an up-to-date analyst's report and an archive of news articles about the company and its competitors. Anybody can get this information. But hardly anybody does.

The same is true with the company's annual report. Getting it is easy. Reading it isn't. The average annual report is so dull it makes the telephone book seem like a page-turner. Nonetheless, knowing the information it contains is a huge advantage.

What you really have to do is to drill down. If you're smart, you get initial data from Bloomberg and then you say, I want to go further. As you dig out more information about the companies strengths and weaknesses, you can extrapolate that data into ideas that make sense.

3. Be accurate. Spell each person's name correctly. Know how to pronounce it. Be certain you've got the title right. More than once, a prospective client has said to me, following what I thought was a reasonably successful meeting, next time you contact me, please use my current title. Making a faux pas like that can cost you the job.

4. Stay focused on the list. This is critical. You have to keep

ters, my missives are neither general nor vague, and they're never about what a great guy I am. They focus on the company by addressing a pinpointed problem.

Why do they work, given that the person who's reading the letter generally has no idea who I am? They work because the executive reading the letter is desperate for ideas.

Coming up with ideas tied to specific problems the company is experiencing requires massive amounts of research. You should know in advance that much of the time, that effort doesn't pay off. But some of the time it does. And when it does, it enables you to create a relationship and sustain it for a long time.

Follow Up

A week or so after you send the letter, make a follow-up phone call. Whether you end up talking directly to the boss or, as is more likely, to the secretary, your message at this point is simple. You have a unique proposition and you want fifteen minutes of the boss's time.

If you happen to get the potential client on the phone, seize the day. Tell her: I can show you how to increase the worth of the company's stock, sell more products, increase productivity, or whatever the issue happens to be.

She has already read your letter, which outlines what you perceive the situation to be. Now you're offering to discuss solutions beyond those mentioned in the letter. The chances are good that she wants to hear what you have to say. So be bold.

Ask directly, when can we schedule a meeting?

Will you get turn-downs? Absolutely. Be prepared. But I want to emphasize that by and large, this method has worked for me. A sizeable percentage of the time, I get hired.

Be Creative

Follow-up does not mean harassing your would-be client with phone calls. You've got to think of creative ways to make contact.

For instance, a potential client contacted us from the West coast and asked us to submit a proposal. We did. In the process, we became enthusiastic about working with this company. After we submitted the proposal, we had a choice: we could sit around passively, waiting for the client to contact us. Or we could find a way to show this client in every possible way that we were interested and that there was some sizzle behind our recommendations.

So my colleagues and I gathered in the conference room and threw around suggestions for follow-up. One idea was to say to the client, we have identified eight trends in your field and we're prepared to share those trends with you as soon as you want to have a meeting.

Someone asked, "What are those trends?" I said, "We'll have to figure them out! That's what research is for."

Another suggestion was to suggest that we have a teleconference. After all, the client was on the West coast. They had no idea who we were. It might be a great idea for them to see us. We could build things into the conference that are so typically New York and so success-oriented that they'd naturally want to be aligned with us. And we could show ourselves to be so warm and supportive and open to the client that they'd naturally want to do business with us.

Doing this involves a number of steps. Calling Kinko's is the first step: They can arrange a teleconference for you.

Then you have to figure out who's going to be in the teleconference, what they're going to say, and what they're going to wear. I recommend rehearsing with talking points and questions so that people will have the correct responses down pat.

I also recommend hiring a producer to position everyone in the proper way.

Again, this may seem like a lot of work. But who would you hire? The agency that sent in a proposal and then sat back waiting? Or the agency that pulled out all the stops?

We got the job.

Brochures, Direct Mail, and Ads

If you're a big company with a huge network and a wide range of services, ads and brochures create a state of awareness.

But if you're an individual entrepreneur operating a small consulting service, an ad may not help. A pamphlet won't help. Direct mail might be instantly discarded.

To get in front of your potential client, you have to use your wits, your charm, maybe your contacts. A compelling letter will get you in the door. A brochure will not.

Your First Meeting

The purpose of this meeting is to get the go-ahead to write a plan of action. To do that, you want to show the person with whom you're meeting that you know what's going on in the organization, that you have easy-to-implement solutions, that you're experienced enough to be trusted.

Vouching for yourself is uncomfortable at best but you have to do it. You can—and should—say, I have consulted in the accounting field or the legal field or the aerospace field, and I know that field better than anybody else. It helps to have a client list of third parties who will endorse you.

Without being this blunt, you have to be able to suggest that the person with whom you're meeting is stuck in a little narrow company, while you bring a whole range of ideas and experience. You have to convince people that you can help them think out of the box.

There are several elements to the first meeting.

Prelude: making small talk. Find a way to make a few seconds of positive small talk. Your goal is to make the other person feel comfortable. So this is not the moment to discuss, say, terrorism. Instead, you might comment on something in his or her office. You might remark on the fact that the other person went to a certain school and you know something about the school. Or you might mention a current sporting event such as the World Series (which is underway as I write). Whatever the topic is, it should be something that puts everybody at ease.

However, don't get stuck there. If the person you're talking to doesn't begin to focus on the purpose of the meeting, it's up to you to turn the conversation in the right direction. You might say, I'm grateful for your time because I believe that our discussion can enhance your company by increasing its stock price, or boosting its sales, or reducing its overhead, or whatever your goal happens to be.

Make sure you state directly that you can help him achieve that goal. Once he hears that, he's going to lean forward. That's your cue to move on to the next part of the meeting.

Act I: asking questions. Start by asking friendly questions, not pejorative or hostile ones. If there are things you need to know, ask now. Also, remember to ask questions that will make the person you're talking to feel good because he can answer them effectively.

For instance, a client of mine was anxious about an upcoming meeting with a man who was crusty and difficult. He asked me, "What do I do?" I said, "Start talking about what you know and in the middle of it stop and ask him a question that you know he can answer successfully. You want him to seem smart in his own eyes when he answers it."

How do you figure out what that question is? Ask a question that teases out information from his field of experience.

In this case, the prospect happened to be in the airline business. When my client asked about airlines, he was thrilled to answer because he knew everything there was to know about airlines. They immediately bonded. By asking the question, my client created a bridge that wasn't there before.

Don't ask questions the prospect can't answer: No one wants to be stumped. And don't even think of asking embarrassing or accusatory questions. You want to be a reassuring presence, not an upsetting one.

You might ask, when you think about other companies in your industry, what are the major areas of competition? When he responds, he'll feel confident about his answer—and he'll have given you two or three additional points of information. (If he can't answer this, he's in the wrong job and you have identified the real reason the company's in trouble.)

The best questions to ask are those relating to your goal. For instance, if you've promised to reduce expenses, ask how are the other companies in your industry cutting costs? Or how have you tried in the past to cut costs?

Then, having asked a question, be quiet. Give him a chance to answer. And give yourself a chance to digest the information before you move to your other questions.

Act II: making your statement. This is the heart of the meeting.

After a few minutes of Q & A, segue into your sales pitch, but try not to have it perceived as such. You've got to convince the person you're meeting with that you understand his problems and his industry, that you have solutions he hasn't considered, that you can help him. At the same time, you don't want to reveal every weapon in your arsenal. So you might indicate something about the general approaches you will use, how long you think it will take to rectify the situation, what you think the benefits might be. Mention enough specifics to whet his appetite.

And don't present your ideas like a waiter reeling off the evening's specials. No one wants to hear a memorized spiel.

Act III: closing the meeting. The ideal way for the meeting to end is for the person you're meeting with to ask for your ideas in writing. This hardly ever happens. So you need to bring it up. Once you've laid out some of your ideas, you might ask, "May I follow up? Can I respond to you in writing?"

Remember: Most people want to say yes. That's why the person you're meeting with agreed to see you in the first place. By saying, I'll get this done for you, you force him either to give you the go-ahead or to say no.

Very few people are going to say no. Once they say yes, you tell them, I'll have a plan of action on your desk within a week. Can I look for a response from you shortly after that? Again, it's easier to say yes.

You have now accomplished two things. You have received the go-ahead for a plan of action. And by building in a whole train of events, you have created a feeling of confidence, a sense that things are already starting to happen.

This is the moment to bring the meeting to a close. If it goes on too long, you'll be drained of your ideas. So keep it short. Close it by saying, "Thank you, I appreciate the time you took and I'll get back to you within a week with a plan for taking this forward."

Now stand up, shake hands, and walk out.

Corporate Politics

At the first meeting, you have to convince the person you're meeting with that you can speak without the hindrance of corporate politics.

People who work inside a corporation assume that they know the corporation better than anybody, so why should they hire a consultant? The answer is easy. There are outside factors influencing the corporation that you may not understand and I can tell you how they affect you.

This approach will work on the West coast, on the East coast, and in the Middle West. It will work in Europe. It will work in Asia.

But in the South and the Southwest, people have ambivalent feelings about consultants. And once you cross into the sovereign state of Texas, you will find an attitude that's downright dismissive.

I particularly enjoy going to Texas and getting assignments for just that reason.

Show Me the Money

Note that you still haven't talked about money. Unless the client brings it up, the first meeting is probably a little early in the game, especially if the client is wavering. However, if the perspective client is desperate to hire you, discuss money now.

How much should you charge? You can charge for your time, for your analysis of a problem, or for the value you create. I prefer the last method. If I can help push a stock up several points, that's a lot of value, and I'm comfortable charging for it. If I can help an executive smooth out difficulties with a spouse—and I've been asked to do this on many occasions—that has a lot of value too. When my clients send me a check, I don't want them thinking that they're paying for my time or my thoughts: I want them to know that they're getting value.

Send a Memo

No matter how your meeting ends—with an agreement to do further business or with a series of mumbled, noncommittal comments—you need to follow up. One way to do this is to give the person something to look at. Unfortunately—as I stated before—leaving behind a brochure won't do. Sooner or later it will get thrown into the trash.

Instead, leave behind a memorandum written with this particular client in mind. It doesn't have to be exhaustive—one or two pages will do—but it has to be directed specifically to the XYZ company and it has to deal with the issues under consideration, whatever they might be.

If you have not gotten the go-ahead for writing a plan of action, sending a memo gives you another chance to hook your potential client.

If you have gotten the go-ahead, you might still want to write the memo. Use the words "Strictly confidential" on the envelope, and send it to the person you met. You can be sure that person will look at it: Everybody wants to see something that's confidential.

At the top of the paper state that this memo is intended to take company XYZ to a level that it doesn't currently enjoy. Then summarize your ideas. Remember: Keep it short. And make certain that every aspect of the memo relates to the company.

This memo will solidify your position.

The Power Behind the Phone

The memo needs to arrive at the office within two or three days of your meeting. If you are also planning to submit a plan of action, the memo needs to arrive a few days prior to that. The whole process shouldn't take more than a week.

During that crucial time, call the secretary regularly to let her know the progress that you're making. Tell her, you'll have something for her boss in short order. You want her to be your ally. Enlist her assistance now.

Don't Write a Proposal

Let me be blunt: Hardly anybody writes proposals and succeeds. Maybe that's because the word proposal sounds tentative. The person reading it is going to think, I suppose I should make a decision. But perhaps I ought to look at other proposals first.

Instead, write a plan of action. It sounds more direct, more effective. If you're presenting someone with a plan of action, you're saying, this is something you can do right now and I can work with you on it.

That semantic shift may sound minor but it produces a more positive, action-oriented mind set.

Writing a Plan of Action

When writing a plan of action, put in defined goals that will benefit the person receiving your plan. You want that person to think, I can look good if this consultant does this for me.

It's best to emphasize actions that will produce immediate results, especially for the person you're working with.

You also want to include the following:

- one or more specific objectives
- an analysis of the company's current situation
- a series of actions that will help the company reach your stated goal by a certain date
- an estimate of how long each action should take
- a discussion of the likely results of each action
- an acknowledgment of possible problems that could arise
- and a clear explanation of your fee and how you expect to receive it

The Art of Making Presentations

When you present the plan of action, try not to send it through the mail. You're better off presenting it in an ordinary meeting.

When you sit down for the first part of the meeting, wait for the other person to speak. If that doesn't happen right away, fine. Let the silence fill the room.

They have invited you in to make your presentation. Since you're not saying anything, they have to do it. The chances are they're going to say something that's positive for you. That's what you want.

That positive statement sets the tone and enables you to start on the best possible note. In my experience, that means jumping to the finish line by stating the ultimate result that you hope to achieve. Try saying something like this:

- I want to put points on the board for XYZ Company
- I can help raise the productivity of XYZ Company
- I can help you navigate through a transition
- I can help you create a product turnaround

You want that headline to be in everyone's mind throughout your presentation. That way, as you discuss your various ideas, everyone knows where you're heading.

As you go through your plan of action, be sure to ask questions. You want to say, Does that work for you? How does that sound to you? Can I have some feedback on that? By asking those questions, you engage the other people in the discussion.

The worst thing to do is to sit down and read through your plan of action while they sit there in judgment. At the end they will say thank you, good-bye, we'll think about it. And you know what that means.

You have to engage them in the process.

Contracts with Clients

A lot of people are reluctant to ask for contracts. I'm not sure why, but I think they're afraid that if they ask for one, the client might back out.

I think they're foolish. A contract is your protection. But I realize that asking for one can be intimidating. This is what I recommend: Instead of whipping out a twenty-page legal document written in six-point type, tell your client that you'd like to formalize your agreement. You can say, I'm going to send you a note and I'd appreciate your acknowldgement of it. That's all you have to do.

The note, which will lay out the terms you have discussed, can be your contract. It should list what you are going to do, how long it will take, how much you expect to be paid, and so on. Be sure that the contract has an exit clause.

You might also include a clause that says this contract will continue for thirty days past the completion date unless canceled by either party in writing. That gives you thirty days to generate more business.

Solving Problems

Once you've written your plan of action and signed the contract, you have to prove yourself by actually solving your client's problem. Doing that requires a mixture of skills. To wit:

- It takes the ability to understand what the problem actually is. That means objectively analyzing the situation by stepping outside your client's range of understanding and being able to offer a new perspective on the situation.
- It takes the courage to be candid about the problems facing the company.
- It takes the creativity to develop a series of possible solutions.
- It takes intelligence and compassion to guide the client through the process. That's not so hard while things are going well. But when you're delivering bad news, it's another story.

Bring in the Hessians

Consultants are like mercenary soldiers: They are hired to perform tasks that no one else wants to touch. They speak the truth, even when it's ugly. That's probably the least enjoyable part of a consultant's job—and the most important. To do it effectively, you have to be soft with the client. When you tell them they have to fire half the people on their payroll, or declare bankruptcy, or do anything else that's unpleasant, it helps to relate a funny story to lighten the burden. You have to convince them, even when things are unimaginably bad, that things are not as bad as they could be. There's a real art to it.

You may be tempted at those moments to emphasize the optimistic view and underplay the negative. Don't do it. The ideal consultant has the courage of his or her convictions and tells the client what the client ought to know.

Keeping the Ball in the Air

One advantage of being a consultant is that each situation is unique, so you're always doing something new. The boredom quotient is low.

One disadvantage is that every time you complete the task for which you were hired, you're out of work.

To keep from being constantly on the job market, you need to turn one-time clients into on-going clients. That process begins with the successful completion of your first assignment. Once you've done that, you've established a platform. You can say to your client, we've got a toehold. Now how do we go to the next level?

In other words, you enter into a process with the client. A process is never completed. If it was, we'd all be in Nirvana, smoking cigars and drinking cognac. In this world, there's always something you can do better. That's the way business is—and it doesn't matter if you're running a mom-and-pop bodega or General Electric.

That's why, with every client I have, I try to meet with them regularly to evaluate what has happened and to look to the future. There's constant reassessment: Here's what worked, here's what didn't work, here are the lessons we learned from it, and here's the plan for the next month or two.

You should always have a clear view of where this client should be in two or three years. In every meeting you should be saying, here's how I can take you forward over the next few weeks toward that vision.

To do that effectively, you need to build upon your successes and accept failure when it comes (because ideas that sound great in the office don't necessarily hold up in the marketplace). You need to think purposefully and creatively. Most of all, you need to make sure that the ball is always in the air.

Back to Emerson

There comes a time in the life of every successful consultant when everything begins to fall into place.

By then you will have learned how to generate work. You will no longer be surprised when new assignments arrive at unexpected times and from unlikely sources. You will know immediately which clients you are going to enjoy working with and which ones are going to cause you trouble. And once you accept a proj-

ect, you will understand intuitively what the next step ought to be
and you will know how to make it happen.

Until then, remember the words of Ralph Waldo Emerson,
who pointed out (in an essay entitled "Wealth") that "good luck is
another word for tenacity of purpose."

8

A PR Primer

A young writer recently got into trouble for being ungracious. Oprah Winfrey had chosen his novel for her book club. Although every single book so designated has become a best seller and made its creator rich, the young author was not happy about it. He felt uncomfortable and ambivalent—would he be taken seriously in the literary world?—and he expressed those feelings to a reporter.

Not surprisingly, his uneasiness soon became public knowledge and he was roundly criticized. Ms. Winfrey withdrew her invitation to appear on the show. Other writers derided him as offensively elitist. An op-ed piece in the *New York Times* heralded him as the "Not-Yet-Ready-for-Prime-Time Novelist" and described the whole brouhaha as one in which the novelist "puts foot in mouth, chews hard, then swallows."

Did sales suffer? Frankly, I don't think they did. But the author's personal reputation certainly did. And although he tried to apologize, apologies—as any PR person could tell you—are always too little, too late.

That's why it's so important to present yourself to the public in the right way, right from the start. You don't need to hire a PR agent to do that. Just use your common sense—and read this chapter.

What Is PR?

Many people think of public relations as a sort of synonym for media exposure. Without a doubt, media exposure is a major concern for people in my field. But PR can also be described more generally as the way the public perceives you, whether you're talking to Oprah or to the person sitting next to you on the train. If you interact with the public on any level, public relations affects you. That's why you need to pay attention to it—even if you've also hired a guy like me to help you out.

How to Develop Your Message

Part of doing your own PR is simply knowing what to say about yourself when the occasion arises. Some people evidently think that the occasion arises whenever another person is in the room. Not so. One of the worst PR mistakes you can make is to talk about yourself all the time. But there are times when you should talk about yourself, and when these situations arise, you need to be prepared. You can do that by writing out three separate spiels about yourself:

The twenty-second elevator speech. Imagine the circumstances. There you are, heading to the twenty-sixth floor, when who should enter the elevator but the very person you have been trying desperately to meet. What should you say?

At that tense moment, you don't have time to compose a speech in your head. It should be there, ready to go: your Twenty-Second Elevator Speech, a nutshell description of your most important qualities and experiences.

The one-minute presentation. Or maybe you're at a convention or a cocktail party, and you figure you can talk about yourself for about a minute. What would you say during those critical sixty seconds? Don't trust yourself to speak extemporaneously: You run the risk of talking for too long or of getting sidetracked. You want to have your one-minute statement permanently filed in your brain, ready to go.

The written essay. Finally, there's the 1,500 word essay, an in-depth story about yourself. I would begin it with eight to ten topic sentences. Think of the topic sentences as headlines, and keep them short and punchy.

Then apply the old-fashioned principles of composition, the ones you learned in school: supply two or three examples to illustrate each topic sentence.

This exercise will organize your thoughts and enable you to talk about yourself at length when the situation calls for it. It also provides a sort of backstory for briefer presentations. Thus, if you need to limit your message to three or four items, you can pick and choose from among the points in your essay.

Recently, for example, a woman came to me to prepare for a television interview. She's a powerful woman, but she was nervous. She asked me, what should I say?

I said, write down three major points you want to make. Then let's put together two examples for each one of those points. That's what you should say about yourself. It's that simple.

She took my suggestion, and her television appearance was a smashing success.

Have ever wondered what kind of advice you might get if you hired a public relations person? Now you know.

Why You Should Do Your Own PR

I once had a highly accomplished client who did remarkable work but was so hesitant to do any form of PR, for reasons that are still a mystery to me, that I don't even feel free to tell you what field he was in. Suffice it to say that had he wanted to be known, he would be famous. And admired.

He came to me because he was involved in a project that ran into difficulties and he wanted the problem to go away. He said, it's your job to keep this out of the press.

I said, okay, we can minimize the damage. But what we really should do is to draw attention to the many successful projects you've worked on that have nothing to do with this catastrophe.

He never accepted that part of the equation. He believed that his work spoke for itself. I said, yes, but if you don't point it out to people, they won't notice it. He said, they will. I said, they won't. We argued back and forth.

Ultimately, it was his call. Which is why you've never heard of this guy.

Even if you feel sympathetic to his approach, you can't afford to emulate him, because PR concerns your reputation, which is constantly in flux, constantly being recreated, whether you do anything about it or not. If you refuse to participate in the process, you risk finding out, too late, that your image has changed and your glorious accomplishments have faded into memory.

You don't want to become someone about whom it might be said, "She used to be quite capable. I don't know what she's doing these days."

Not after fifty, you don't.

If you still have a hankering for recognition, if success in the world still means something to you, then refusing to do your own PR is a huge mistake.

The Ten Commandments of Public Relations

I don't compare myself to Moses, but I do know something about PR. These are the basic rules:

Commandment Number 1: Have a Clear Message

What do you want to impart to people about yourself or your business? It can't be ten different things. A message that complicated distorts the process and is too much for people to absorb. To do effective PR, for yourself or for anybody else, you have to limit yourself to three or four messages, tops.

You might, for instance, want people to think of you as industrious, honest, and an expert in your field. You might want to be viewed as someone who can motivate others. You might want to be seen as an original thinker or a compelling leader or someone with an uncanny grasp of the economy. These are important messages and they can be very effective, assuming you obey the next two commandments.

Commandment Number 2: Support Your Message With Examples

If you pride yourself on being able to get the job done on time, even under intense pressure, you better have several examples of how you did just that.

If you want to be known as someone who can motivate people, you have to have examples of how you've increased productivity where you've worked in the past.

In short, you had better be able to prove your case.

Commandment Number 3: Remember Your Audience

To craft an effective message, make sure the messages you choose resonate with your audience. Observe them carefully and consider the qualities that matter to them—not just to you.

I know a widely-published professor who had a year-long appointment at an ivy league university, at the end of which he was to be granted tenure. During the year, he spoke at international conferences. He wrote for a prestigious journal. His students gave him a standing ovation at the end of the term, and he dazzled the faculty with his artistic, linguistic, and culinary talents, none of which had anything to do with his major field of expertise. Yet despite his efforts, he didn't get tenure.

Why? Because what people say they want is not necessarily what they really want. Sure, if you had asked the faculty, they would probably have said they were looking for someone who was a brilliant scholar and a charismatic teacher. The professor was trying to give exactly them that. His message was clear: I am a star.

Unfortunately, that message did not resonate with his audience. They didn't want a star. They didn't want to feel upstaged. They wanted a colleague, a committee member, someone who would fit seamlessly into their community. A better message would have been "I am a team player."

Commandment Number 4: Repeat Your Message Again and Again

Take it from me, the PR you do on Tuesday is forgotten on Wednesday. To drive your message home, your campaign has to last over an extended period of time. Otherwise your message won't sink in. Unless you can provide people with repeated examples of what you're doing, you will fail to make an impression. People forget.

If you have any question about that, conduct a little test right now. Ask yourself, What was on the front page of the newspaper one week ago? Or how about this: What was on the television news two nights ago? Very few people can answer either question.

Plus, you've got to remember that you're dealing with the passing parade. The group you're communicating with today will have an entirely different composition two years from now.

So you've got to repeat your message over and over, in different ways. One iteration is never enough.

Commandment Number 5: Establish Yourself as an Expert

Are you an expert on crisis management, on maritime law, on antiquarian books, or, for that matter, on anything at all? If so, you're in an ideal position to do your own PR.

Just the other day, a fellow called us. He said that in this current economy, there are going to be more bankruptcies than ever and I know how to help companies who are facing that problem.

None of my clients is close to bankruptcy, but he put the idea in my head, and I made an appointment to talk with him. I may never need to recommend his services. But if I do, I'll call him. Because even though I know plenty of lawyers and accountants who are knowledgeable about the intricacies of bankruptcy proceedings, this guy has established himself as an expert in my mind. I'd call him first.

The trouble with being a generalist is that it means you're almost never the perfect person for the job. By becoming an expert at something, you become the perfect person.

Many people resist this idea because they are afraid of getting pigeon-holed. They think that if they become an expert on, say, growing organic lettuce, they'll never be allowed to talk about the rest of the vegetable kingdom. Actually, it's the other way around: By concentrating your expertise, you give your professional life a focus.

In my profession, for instance, I concentrate on the public relations needs of CEOs around the world. Sure, I have clients who don't fit that category. But the bulk of my work comes to me because I have established my expertise in a certain area.

To establish yourself as an expert, you need to give your work a focus. You need to have the courage to proclaim yourself an expert. And you need to be able to back up your claim.

One way to do that is to act upon the corollary to this commandment.

Corollary to Commandment Number 5: Create a Newsletter

There is no easier, faster way to establish your credentials as an expert than producing a newsletter that puts out information other people can use. And it doesn't matter what your field is.

If I ran a janitorial service, for instance, I would send out a regular newsletter about trends in cleaning. If I owned a shoe store, I'd develop a newsletter about shoes. If I was a waiter, I'd create a newsletter about trends in eating out.

Do I follow my own advice? In this case, yes. Since my work focuses on the business community, I've developed a newsletter about the issues that are of concern to them: Mainly social, economic, and political trends. It's called the *Dilenschneider Trend Forecasting Report*. It comes out in January and September, enabling me to keep in contact with about 2,000 people.

That may not sound like a lot. But people regularly quote from the *Dilenschneider Trend Letter,* often verbatim. Just the other day, I talked to a man who said he'd like 500 copies of the *Trend Letter* to send to his clients. And last year, Paine Webber used several parts of the *Trend Letter* in presentations all over the world. I couldn't have hoped for a better third-party endorsement.

Another benefit of writing the *Trend Letter* is that it creates a dialogue with my clients. I've found that the real indication of whether or not people read it is whether they contact me to argue about it.

For instance, take global warming. I think it's a problem. That hole in the ozone layer worries me. But many people think those concerns are misguided. Every year, I get letters from representatives of big oil companies arguing with me.

Same thing happens with the Japanese business community. Every year, evidently, I get something wrong. Every year, they send people to see me so we can discuss it.

Does this please me? You bet. I'm always willing to consider the evidence and I'm happy to engage in a debate. It involves everyone in a constructive exchange.

Besides, it's great PR.

Commandment Number 6: Control Your Output

As many a beleaguered celebrity and public official can attest, it's easy to lose control over your message, and once that has happened, it's hard to get it back. That's why it's important to try to do whatever you do in as controlled a way as possible, especially when you're dealing with media or the public.

For instance, maybe you're going to give a speech. You need to make certain that every aspect of your presentation, from the way you dress to the way you answer questions at the end, supports your overall message.

Maybe you need to clear up a misunderstanding. You could leave a message over the phone, but we all know how dangerous that is. Or you could write a letter. That way, you take control of your own communication.

When you give a speech, write an article, or send someone a letter, you take control of your own message. That's a good thing.

Commandment Number 7: Have Someone Else Do It for You

I don't mean hire someone. I mean that the most desirable PR always comes from someone else's mouth. You need a third party to sing your praises.

Of course, we all know people who are only too happy to do it themselves. They do it incessantly—in conversation, in writing, and even in interior decoration. My favorite expression of the how-great-I-am syndrome is the love-me room, which is invariably decorated with degrees and awards and trophies and framed book jackets and photographs of the Great One hobnobbing with celebrities or bowing to the Queen, all vivid ways of showing how important they are. I guess this is their way of reinforcing themselves.

I have to say, some people evidently succeed by doing this. You've probably spent as many miserable hours in their company as I have. But I persist in believing that the same folks would be more successful—not to mention more popular—if they could only quiet down. Bragging is not good PR.

Having other people talk about you in a positive way is good PR. The third party is extremely important.

That's why artists, actors, and writers have agents. That's why the best way to meet someone is to get somebody else to introduce you and the best way to get a job is to be recommended.

And that's why there is ultimately nothing more important in terms of PR than your network.

Commandment Number 8: Expand Your Network

New York's Shea Stadium is named after a great man named Bill Shea, who ran a law firm called Shea and Gould. He was the king of the networkers. On his desk he kept seven or eight huge Rolodexes filled with names and addresses from all over the country. His assistant kept the information up to date so that Bill could keep in constant contact with these people. His networking skills enabled him to become a very powerful person.

It's never too late to expand your own network. After all, this is not something to do once in a while. You need to do it all the time. The number one way is by going to events. Go to trade associations, professional events, conferences. Attend university events, charity functions, and community meetings. Be visible.

And talk to everyone. When you meet people, think about how they fit into your design for going forward—and think about what you can do to help them. (For suggestions on how to start a conversation, see Chapter 10.)

After you meet someone, you can write a letter that says I met you at the church festival last week. I found our conversation about such-and-such quite fascinating and I'd like to continue it. May I call you? Most people are flattered.

Don't be heavy-handed about expanding your network, though. I've seen people do that firsthand. My wife and I like to throw big parties. More than once, I've had people call me afterwards to ask for a list of every person who attended. I always demur. It's an embarrassing moment.

On the other hand, people come to parties at my house and meet other guests and get together afterwards, and I think that's fine. That's the way it should be.

Another way to network is to get the people you already know to introduce you to the people you want to know. To do this, you have to ask, and that's not easy. But you have to do it.

For instance, let's say you're looking for a job. And let's say you've done some volunteer work for the Cancer Society. I guarantee you, someone you've worked with there can introduce you to the members of the board of the Cancer Society, who undoubtedly include some influential people. It's hard to make such a request. But it's an easy way to expand your network and get some great advice.

Finally, there's one other way to expand your network, and it's the easiest of all. Be nice. To everyone. From the moment you get up to the moment you go to bed, you probably have dozens of interactions that you don't normally record: with people over the phone, people who come to the door, people on the street, people at lunch. If you're decent to these people and you keep an eye out for how you can help them, your network will expand.

The word "networking" has come to have a negative tinge because it has been associated with ambitious, status-conscious careerists who only care what you can do for them. People who go about networking in that way ultimately make very few solid connections.

Building a network in the right way means being willing to go beyond yourself.

Commandment Number 9: Follow Up

Return your phone calls. Write thank you notes. Reciprocate. And do it with dispatch.

Obvious advice? Obviously. But too many people don't do it.

For instance, I met an interior decorator at a dinner party about a year ago It was fascinating sitting next to her and I told her how much I enjoyed it. I also told her that I knew a couple who had just purchased an enormous house. I said, I know they would benefit from working with someone of your abilities. Please call me and I'll put you in touch with them.

Four or five months later, she called. By then it was too late. The moral is clear: Follow up—and do it quickly.

Commandment Number 10: Use the Media to Your Advantage

There's a maxim that as long as they spell my name correctly, any PR is good PR. I don't agree. If the press writes a negative story about you, that's not good. You have to be careful about how you expose yourself to the press and what you say in the presence of a reporter, something the young novelist I discussed at the top of this chapter seemed to forget.

Many people have the notion that it would be great to get a story into the press about themselves. In my view, you never want to get a story into the press about yourself. That's because good reporters strive for balance and objectivity. So if a reporter writes a story about you, it will mention your failings as well as your accomplishments, quote your detractors, and remind everyone of that long-ago scandal. That kind of coverage—the only kind you're going to get in a halfway respectable publication—is not going to help you, because people tend to remember the negatives more than the positives.

The best way to appear in the press is to comment about a topic, never about yourself. That way, even if people disagree with you, you're engaged in a legitimate argument over a point of view. You are not the center of attention. And yet attention naturally flows to you. It's a PR coup.

Using the Media

You don't need to be well-known to use the media. You just have to be savvy.

Let's say, for instance, that you're an expert in library science or bilingual education or the housing needs of the elderly. (That is, you're a librarian, a teacher, or a real estate broker.) You can go on the internet, do a search, and get the names of scores—make that hundreds—of writers who have addressed that topic in the last year.

You'll know where they are, how to spell their names, what they wrote about. Then you can write them a letter. I'd say, I admired your recent piece in the *Arizona Republic.* Your analysis impressed me and I wonder if you've considered such-and-such. You might offer them a relevant anecdote from your experience or a piece of information they didn't know.

They may not answer your letter. Don't let that bother you. Next time they run a related story, send another letter. Your aim is to establish yourself as an expert, a source of information. If your letters are thoughtful, sooner or later the reporter is likely to contact you.

Or consider writing letters to the editor. Every time there's a newspaper story about your topic, write a letter to the editor. There are basic rules for writing letters to the editor. We all know them:

- A letter to the editor has to be short and to the point
- It has to be timely
- And it has to present a point of view that is different from the opinion expressed in the original article

Admittedly, it is difficult—though not impossible—to get letters to the editor published in prestigious papers like the *New York Times* or the *Washington Post.* It can be easier to break into smaller papers. Fortunately, it doesn't matter where your letter is published. Because afterwards, you can Xerox it and send it to your network with a brief note. The *Citizen Register* took the time to publish this letter, you can say. I think this topic is extremely important, and I thought you'd be interested too. Any comments? You'll get comments back and that creates a dialogue.

Anybody can do this.

Appearing on talk radio is something else almost anybody can do. You can certainly call call-in shows, although I don't necessarily recommend that. Or you can find out who the producer of the show is and contact that person. If you present yourself as someone with expertise and a point of view, the producer may be interested.

One of the easiest ways to get on the air is to write a book. Send it to radio and TV stations along with a set of questions you can answer.

You can also appear on television shows. But don't do it if you don't look good. I don't mean you have to look like a movie star. But you have to look okay.

If you do end up on television, please dress appropriately. Men look better in a jacket and tie. Women look better in a suit or a dress. Avoid complicated prints. Avoid casual clothes. Don't look like you're dressed for the *Jerry Springer Show*, even if you are.

One of the great things about radio and television is that their needs are inexhaustible. They have to put guests on the air all the time. If you're inventive enough, you ought to be able to figure out a way to take advantage of that.

If you find yourself going on TV, the most important person to talk to is not the host. It's the camera man. Get there early so you can talk to him about getting the most flattering camera angle. If you've got a weight problem—and remember, TV will exacerbate that—try to get a head-and-shoulders shot.

Finally, if you're anxious, contact a media coach. Some of them are pretty good. But many are hacks who will try to change you. Don't let them do it. You are who you are and you want to express your point of view.

PR Don'ts

There are certain dangers inherent in doing your own PR. Most of them can be avoided. Here are PR's dirty dozen for the over-fifty crowd:

Bad taste. I think that speaks for itself.

Trying too hard. Calling someone repeatedly or communicating without a valid reason is a mistake. If people don't respond after two or three well-spaced attempts, back off.

Insulting people. Insulting somebody, even subtly, is a mistake, and sometimes it can be a worse one than you realize. The person you insult, however inadvertently, may say nothing to you. But they could denigrate you to everyone they know. They could even repeat your remark, allowing an insult to one person to ripple out and insult an entire network. That's not a good thing.

Lying. The problem with lying is that when people find out about it—and they do—no one will ever trust you again.

A friend of mine encouraged a mutual acquaintance to see a film called *Run, Lola, Run.* Our acquaintance rented the film from Blockbuster but never got around to watching it. Nonetheless, he wrote my friend a letter in which he said that *Run, Lola, Run* was a great film. Thrilled, my friend immediately called to discuss the film in detail. "Did you like that scene halfway through?" he asked. But our acquaintance couldn't relate to it. He was caught in a lie.

That was a bad mistake. It had repercussions. Yet it was entirely avoidable.

Opportunism. Being opportunistic at the wrong time can turn a viable business prospect into a PR catastrophe. The appearance of benefiting from someone else's misfortune makes people queasy and can besmirch your reputation. Don't do it.

Presenting yourself poorly. If you come across as a slob, people will think of you that way. If you *seem* disorganized, people will assume that you *are* disorganized. As you should know by now, everyone judges a book by its cover. Present yourself according.

Writing badly. Be judicious in your writing. Use the spell check. And proofread everything you intend to send, preferably by printing it out and reading a hard copy. It's amazing how easy it is to miss the most blatant errors when you're reading them on a computer screen.

If you're unsure of writing fundamentals, show your résumé and any important letters to someone whose editing skills you trust.

Finally, read *The Elements of Style* by William Strunk Jr. and E. B. White or, for a more contemporary take, *Woe is I: The Grammarphobe's Guide to Better English in Plain English* by Patricia T. O'Conner.

Being bigoted. Making ethnic jokes, racial slurs, or sexist comments is never okay, even when you think it is. Not only is it the wrong thing to do, but from the PR standpoint, it's a disaster. I'll never forget eating dinner with a group of high-ranking military officers in San Antonio. As we walked out of the restaurant, a United States Army colonel made a joke about the African American waiters. It was greeted with dead silence. A few minutes later, the general said, I've had a lot of black soldiers under my command and some of them died for their country.

He never said, that was the wrong thing to say. But he left that point on the table. Making bigoted remarks is not only immoral— it's just plain dumb.

Associating with negative symbols. Many people drink, but associating yourself with alcohol is not smart. You don't want people to be reminded of you every time they see a vodka ad.

The same is true with tobacco. Many people smoke, but you don't want people thinking of you every time they see a pack of Marlboro Lights.

I'm not saying you can't indulge in those activities. But I think it's smart to wait for someone else to recommend them first, particularly when you're looking for a job or otherwise trying to impress.

People judge you by what you do, where you do it, and whom you do it with. So be aware.

Being out of date. A lot of older people don't understand new trends and are not interested in them, especially when they involve music and television. For example, *The Simpsons* has been a top-rated show since 1989. Just now, I asked a fifty-seven-year-old friend of mine if he'd ever seen it. The answer? No.

That's a mistake.

Different generations have different concerns. You can start a conversation with anyone in my generation by asking, where were you when John F. Kennedy was shot? But the business world is filled with heavy-hitters who weren't even born in 1963. No point in asking the question.

If you're going to talk about events from your youth—I would avoid it if possible—you've got to relate them to the present. Otherwise, it's just an exercise in nostalgia, which is never interesting to anyone who wasn't there.

I take as my model an Englishman named Alan Campbell Johnson who'd been with Mountbatten in India. After World War Two, he handled the transfer of power from the British to the Indians. When he discussed that period of time, he never spoke about how great he was, although he was. He talked about what we had learned and how it could be applied to international situations today. He wasn't reliving the past; he was applying the lessons of the past to the present. That's a very different thing.

Being bitter. It's understandable that people over fifty sometimes feel bitter. Letting it show, however, is a mistake. I remember counseling a man who came in wanting a job. His first comment was that he figured he was too old and didn't have much of a chance but he was going to try anyway.

That was a strike against him. Making a comment like that is, at best, pointless. At worst, it introduces the thought that maybe you *are* too old. My advice: Keep those thoughts to yourself.

Trying to hide your age. Trying to look good for your age is a worthy goal; being coy about your age or pretending to be significantly younger than you actually are is a mistake.

Sooner or later, you'll slip up and your true age will be revealed—whereupon it will become a topic of conversation. Avoid that embarrassment entirely by being, if not forthcoming, then at least not dishonest about your age.

Spin vs. Substance

In the last decade or so, public relations has come under criticism, thanks to the notorious concept of spin. But spin, no matter how expertly done, eventually comes to a sputtering halt.

What matters is substance. You have to have something to say. You have to develop expertise. You have to be associated with something that matters.

That's the key to doing your own PR.

9

Bridging the Generation Gap

"Old Age and Youth cannot live together," wrote Shakespeare, who lived at a time when fifty was considered old.

Sometimes, it seems to me, they can't *work* together either. The assumptions and experiences of the Baby Boomers, now in their forties and fifties, and the so-called Silent Generation, which preceded the Boom, differ dramatically from those of Generation-X and the yet-to-be-named generations snapping at their heels. Those differences create tension.

In the past, all this had relatively little impact in the workplace because each generation was locked into its own organizational stratum. Top management slots were filled by the most experienced people, who were invariably the oldest; middle management positions were filled by the next generation; entry-level jobs went to the youngest generation. You started on the bottom when you were young and spent the rest of your career "climbing the corporate ladder." It was that simple.

In many companies today, that ladder has been kicked aside and the rigid hierarchies of the past have been overturned. In addition, young entrepreneurs in their thirties and even in their twenties have altered the business landscape by building companies that are immune to the old rules. So things are different. Older people may have more experience and a greater sense of loyalty, but younger people have an edge they didn't have in the past. Not only are they more flexible and energetic, the eternal attributes of youth, they are vastly more knowledgeable in one essential area—technology. That gives them a serious advantage.

Young people today are not afraid to ask for what they want, and they have high expectations. In fact, according to a survey of college seniors taken by KPMG International, 74 percent of them believe that they will become millionaires.

Plus, they expect to get there in record time. I wouldn't be surprised if a sizeable number of them expect to reach that goal by age thirty.

Neither my generation nor the Baby Boomers entertained expectations like that. Those of us who aspired to become part of the establishment—far from a universal goal in the 1960s and 1970s—thought it would take a while. We figured that we'd follow the rules and if we were up to snuff, the rewards would come in due time.

Generation-Xers don't want to wait. And who can blame them?

Generational Stereotypes

Ever since Tom Brokaw wrote a book about the men and women who fought in World War II and titled it *The Greatest Generation* (a term immediately embraced by all to whom it applied), subsequent generations have taken a beating. Unless you happen to be a member of that exalted generation, don't expect to hear anything good about yourself.

Thus people my age, born just before the Baby Boomers, are generally characterized as dull conformists (unless they qualify as members of the Beat Generation, in which case they are considered conformists of another sort). Baby Boomers are viewed as self-satisfied egotists. Generation-Xers are seen as apolitical slackers who mistake irony for intelligence. One way or another, everybody gets slammed.

In the real world, that kind of stereotyping—like any other kind—won't wash. No single individual embodies all the clichés of a generation. Still, there are generational differences. So let me begin with the harshest of them: The younger generation thinks you're old. And they're right. They think you look tired, out of shape, and pathetically out of style. They're dismissive of your musical tastes and contemptuous of your computer skills. If you come from the generation before the Baby Boom, they think you're authoritarian, conservative, and way too enamored of World War Two and the heroes of the past. They don't want to hear another word about Winston Churchill or the Brooklyn Dodgers.

If you're a Baby Boomer, you get a flogging that's more severe. Ever wonder why younger people are so pessimistic and cynical? It's because of you! Young people think that you're self-aggrandizing, self-righteous, self-indulgent, and probably to blame for every major problem facing us today. You could have become enlightened. You could have cleaned up the environment and changed the world. But you didn't. Instead, according to a thirty-year-old newspaperman of my acquaintance, you became just another boring businessperson obsessed with PowerPoint displays and contemporary business clichés. (In contrast, he noted, members of the Greatest Generation make statements that mean something.)

And by the way, members of Generation-X do not want to hear another word about the 1960s, much as they envy you for having lived through that tumultuous era. Anything you might say about those fraught, unforgettable times only hurts you because it reminds them that you're a sell-out. After all, once upon a time you had ideals. But Baby, look at you now.

There is not a lot you can do to change these views. Even responding to such criticisms plays against you, as I realized the other night when I watched several beleaguered Baby Boomers valiantly trying to stand up for themselves. The thirty-year-old at the table looked at me wryly. "Note the defensiveness of the Baby Boom Generation," he said.

Yet the younger generation wants everything that you want, including love, money, personal fulfillment, and success in their chosen fields. They just don't want to wait for it the way you did.

Your job, if you want to get along with them, is to help them get what they want—not to prove how misguided they are. The first step in the process is to understand something about them.

Mission impossible? Not at all.

How to Get Along With Younger Generations

Sooner or later, you will find yourself having a professional discussion with someone who is twenty-five or thirty years younger than you, young enough to be your child. And yet you will be talking to that person as an equal.

That person could be your customer, your client, even your supervisor. That person could be someone you're interviewing or someone who's interviewing you. Here's how to hit it off:

Don't patronize. Don't pander. They can see through that kind of condescension, and they don't like it.

At the same time, recognize that young people need encouragement, sometimes in ways that will strike you as distressingly childish. A museum official put it this way:

> Muhammad Ali once described someone by saying, "He has some maturities on him." I think of that often because I've noticed that young people, especially the men, need more attention than older people and are more demanding. Right now, I'm working with two people who are installing a new exhibit. The younger one, who's in his mid-twenties, has a strong need for personal attention and constant interaction. Last week, he literally asked me to watch him do something and then take his picture while he was doing it. The other one, who's about ten years older, only consults me when he needs direction. He respects the fact that I'm going to make the final decision, the considered judgment. He doesn't waste my time. He's got some maturities on him.

Nonetheless, she gives the younger employee a good deal of attention. She figures—and I think she's right—that it'll pay off in the long run. When dealing with young people, it's important to withhold judgment and make that investment.

Understand that by virtue of living over half a century, you have gained a historical viewpoint. Within your field, for instance, you have some idea of what has worked and what hasn't. You know that some efforts sound good but fail miserably while others are hugely effective but take time. You know that traumatic events can throw everything into chaos. And you know that, as a rule, chaos subsides and order returns. Young people don't—can't—know that.

The movements of history are also unknown to many young people. Even those who have studied history—a distressingly small number, as far as I can see—lack a visceral understanding of its rhythms.

In the weeks following the events of September 11, young people were profoundly shaken. In an article in the *New York Times,* reporter Jane Gross addressed this phenomenon. She pointed out that the Greatest Generation remembers Hitler. Baby Boomers remember air-raid drills and the Cuban Missile Crisis. But Generation-X experienced none of those calamitous public traumas, and as a result, many were unprepared to deal with our latest one.

If you're in touch with young people, part of your role is helping them understand the forces of history and come to grips with the realities of our time.

Don't try to fit into their milieu. I don't mean you should avoid their milieu. On the contrary: I recommend seeking out their milieu. But pretending that you belong there, hoping that they'll see you as one of them, will only earn their contempt. Better to think of yourself as a tourist in the country of the young.

Once in a while, when I'm in the city late after a television appearance, I'll stop in at a club on the way home. I'll sit at the bar and have a cup of coffee and chat with the young people milling around. I don't know whether it's the music or the conversation, but I am always stunned to realize how different their perspective is from mine. Being with them, in however casual a way, helps me feel more in touch. I know many uptight business executives, dark blue suit types, who would never do that, and I think it stultifies their lives and their careers.

Build their confidence. To do that, you need to understand that no matter how confident young people pretend to be, they are riddled with insecurities, even when they are hugely successful. You have to be able to deal with those doubts.

One way to help them feel more confident is to share your knowledge. Many times, younger people are put into supervisory positions by top managers and urged to fly on their own.

Unfortunately, they don't have the depth of experience to do that. When you see a young person in that position, you have an opportunity to help. First, understand that you're not in the running for that job, whether you want it or not. So you're not a threat. Second, recognize that you have an opportunity to transfer your experience to the younger person in a way that may ultimately help you. I've seen it happen.

I knew a wonderful older man at an insurance company who had a supervisor almost thirty years younger than himself. Some older people in that situation might feel bitter. This man took the opposite approach. He assisted the younger man every step of the way, never seeking praise for himself, always seeking to advance the other fellow. Over the years, these two men forged a bond, with the older man imparting to the younger man everything he knew about business. In time the younger man became the company CEO. When that happened, he took excellent care of the older man.

That's not a reason the reason to extend yourself. You should do it because it's the right thing to do. Still, it's nice to know that doing the right thing sometimes pays off.

Understand that what motivates young people is not what motivates you. For instance, you may be motivated by working with a team. Younger people may find it more exciting to work independently. Your goals, interests, and turn-offs are not theirs. And it's a sad fact that the stories it has taken you a lifetime to accumulate are of little interest to the younger generation.

I know a man in his seventies who still has not figured this out, even though he has ten children in their teens and twenties. He's a wonderful story teller, a real raconteur. I sit in rapt attention when he talks. His children listen politely—that's the way they were raised—and leave the room at the first possible moment. They resent his need to be the center of attention, and they don't relate to the stories he tells.

That doesn't have to happen. Stories told in a vacuum drive young people crazy. They don't want to hear about it. On the other hand, they're hungry for ways to think about their own lives and challenges. That's why stories you tell young people should always relate to the present. If there's something in it for them, they'll listen.

Recognize that younger people want to do things fast. They seek instant gratification. You've learned the importance of patience and deliberation. They have not. If you insist upon doing things your way, you'll be happy, but they'll be hopping up and down with frustration. Neither of you will benefit.

I'm sympathetic to the young in this regard, because I remember when I was a young man in a hurry. I wanted to open new offices and hire people and offer new services, and I drove my boss crazy. He repeatedly told me not to push him. I felt that my ideas were good ones, and it frustrated me to be dismissed so cavalierly—so I kept trying. In response, he would occasionally tell me to do a quality assurance study, or to get a second or third opinion, or even to write a paper on one of my ideas. This truly frustrated me. I didn't want to write a paper. I wanted to see my idea bear fruit in the real world. There was a serious standoff between the two of us.

In retrospect, I can see what a pain in the neck I probably was. I can also see how he could have dealt with me more effectively. All he had to do was to sit down and talk with me about my ideas and their consequences. Had he done that, I believe I would have understood that the implications of these ideas were more multidimensional that I realized. We never had those discussions, and so I became resentful and it was a problem.

Today, I meet plenty of young people who are eager to leap into the fire, and I'm the one who has to slow them down. The way to do that, I have learned, is to respond immediately. So I generally suggest that we go downstairs, have a cup of coffee, and discuss the idea. I say, you've got the kernel of something important here, let's see if we can make it work. In the process of having that discussion, we both generally learn whether there is something there. And frequently they come to the conclusion that there's nothing there. Which is fine. But if you don't discuss it with them, you don't get to that point of resolution.

Listen. Consider the possibility that, despite their inexperience, young people might actually have something to say. My sixteen-year-old son, Geoffrey, has complained that older people seldom recognize that fact. "They believe that kids don't have opinions," he told me. "It's really aggravating. They think I'm not old enough to think. Excuse me? I'm thinking! Hello!"

Unfortunately, listening has become a lost art. Most people don't understand that there's strategy and skill in simply listening to what people say. They want to do all the talking.

To get along with younger people, you have to stifle that urge. I believe that it's important for me to sit with my two sons and their friends and listen to what's on their minds. Sounds easy. It's not, because when Froot Loops are getting scattered across the table, you automatically want to pick them up. The minute you do so, the conversation ends.

In the workplace, where your younger colleagues are in their twenties and thirties, Froot Loops are presumably not an issue. But the same rules apply. You need to listen with an open mind. You need to postpone your urge to make momentous pronouncements or to lob small criticisms their way—and that includes criticisms couched as suggestions. You need to listen without judgment.

Ask questions. Deep in their hearts young people recognize that they don't know it all. The best way to help them is to ask a series of constructive questions about who they are and what they want to do. Then let them reach their own conclusions.

Young people will benefit from this because, if you ask questions in the right way, they will be encouraged to consider various courses of action. You will benefit too because talking to young people about their lives (and the lives of their friends) can be unbelievably illuminating.

I remember talking with a wealthy, successful, thoroughly confused twenty-something. Her father had arranged the meeting in hopes that I could help her figure out what lay ahead for her.

She and I met for breakfast at a restaurant on the ground floor of the building where I work. I told her that every New Year's Eve I sit down and make a list of my goals and priorities. I asked, what would you write down if you were going to make such a list?

She couldn't answer that question but it led us into a discussion that helped her focus. I know she left that meeting feeling good about it because between the time when I left the restaurant and the time when I arrived at my office, which is on the twenty-sixth floor, she had called her father on her cell phone and he had called me to say what a terrific meeting it was. I was happy and relieved.

However, I will admit that during the meeting itself, I was careful to order a cappuccino rather than my usual glass of juice. I didn't want her to think I was too, too uncool.

Never betray their confidences. I work with a lot of young people, some of whom are quite prominent. I always begin by telling them that I will never betray their confidences. You and I can discuss any issue under the sun, I say. If you need to talk in the middle of the night, if some terrible problem is weighing you down, I'm here to help. I will work through the matter with you and it will never become public knowledge. I maintain strict confidentiality.

That declaration helps to build a bond of trust.

Keep up. This is an essential part of getting along with the young. You have to be tuned in to the present. In my mind, that's a 24/7 process.

One aspect of keeping up is media awareness, beginning with newspapers and magazines. I try to read a wide variety of periodicals. They include, among others, the *New York Times,* the *Wall Street Journal, Barron's, USA Today,* the *Village Voice, Foreign Affairs, Sports Illustrated, Fortune, Business Week, Fast Company,* and the *Utne Reader,* which offers a collection of articles from the alternative press.

I try to flip through *U.S. News and World Report, Time,* and *Newsweek* every week. I start from the back. I read the daily papers closely, so I skip the news summaries in the front. But the back of the book often contains deeper, more thoughtful stuff and I think that's one way to keep up.

I also try to be aware of what's on the best seller lists, what's hot on Broadway, what the significant art shows in town are. I make an effort to catch the majority of the movies that receive Oscar nominations. I try to watch major television shows, at least once. I even keep up with popular music. Not that it's difficult: My twelve-year-old son, Peter, has definite opinions on the subject and he keeps me up to date.

Another important way of keeping up has to do with talking to people—lots and lots of people.

I talk to strangers all the time. For example, when I go to the Yankee game, I make a point of visiting with the security guard and of having a beer in the Yankee Club with a bunch of fans who are probably truck drivers. I will ask what's going on in their lives. That may sound like an intrusive question, but I assure you, most people seem happy to answer it. I ask questions all the time of people who are outside of my usual sphere. I talk to people in planes, trains, and automobiles, not to mention elevators. Yesterday, for instance, I talked to a messenger in the elevator. I asked him what it was like going between tall buildings in a time of heightened security and he gave me his point of view, which was interesting—and not what I would have expected. I also asked him what he was listening to on his headphones, and he answered that too.

Tap the power of biography. Young people want role models, though they seldom admit to it. That role model might be you— but unless you are one impressive human being, it might not be. A better bet for them is to find a public figure, someone they can read about and emulate, if only in a limited fashion.

Recently I spoke to a young woman about the late Katherine Graham, publisher of the *Washington Post.* Kay Graham arrived at a place in life that was extraordinary for her generation and she did it with style and conviction. The young woman wasn't convinced. She said, "I'm not Katherine Graham."

I said, "That's right. But you can learn some lessons from Katherine Graham." Reluctantly, the young woman agreed to read *Personal History,* Graham's Pulitzer Prize-winning autobiography. We went through the whole book and literally picked out a dozen lessons that were helpful for this individual.

I also know a young man who wanted to be a heavy hitter in the area of venture capital technology. I said, let's dissect the life of Warren Buffett. Oh, no, he said. He didn't want to be like Buffett.

I said, I know that. But Buffett conducted himself in ways that are important for you to understand. For example, Buffett chose to invest in staples, items everyone wanted to have like Coca-Cola or razor blades. In his business life, he made it a point to give responsibility to others. He kept checks on them, but he also empowered them. Those are two lessons you can apply in your own life.

I guess I convinced him, because this guy literally went out and bought all the books about Warren Buffett he could find. He didn't try to develop himself as Warren Buffett—that wasn't his goal—but I'd say he was influenced by seven or eight ideas that Buffett used to guide his life and his business. Reading the book was a thought-provoking experience.

Accept the changing of the guard. That means being willing to help younger people succeed, even when they're placed in positions above you—a situation that's as awkward for them as it is for you. I know of a company that recently went through a period of upheaval. In the midst of it, a group of older people walked into the younger supervisor's office and, to his astonishment, announced that they were there to help. We have some ideas to offer, they said, but we want you to know that, whether you accept them or not, we're behind you. The younger person was knocked off his chair. He accepted their help; they accepted his authority; the company flourished.

Mentoring

One of the best ways to connect with the younger generation is to become a mentor to a younger person. Another way to do it is to allow a younger person to become a mentor to you. Either way, mentoring is a time-honored way to impart information and to connect one generation with the next.

When I graduated from Notre Dame with my Bachelor of Arts degree, I didn't know what to do. So I asked my father. We sat in my bedroom late one night and he said to me, you have three choices. You can join the army. I can help get you a job in a local department store selling shoes. Or you can go to graduate school.

That made it easy. I said, I want to go to graduate school. My father then suggested I talk to a journalism professor named Walter Seifert. So one day I showed up at his house. My timing wasn't good: Seifert's daughter was preparing for her wedding, and everyone was involved in a rehearsal. He didn't even invite me in.

He just met me in the driveway, handed me a stack of papers he had written, and said, I don't have a lot of time to spend with you, but take these and read them.

Spurred on by the less-than-thrilling options my dad had laid out, I read everything Seifert gave me. When I went back to see him, we developed a relationship that lasted until his death. (In fact, I gave the eulogy at his funeral.) As my first mentor, he propelled me into my career. Even as I became more seasoned in my business, I continued to ask him for advice. He made a huge impact on my life, and I'll never forget him.

After I started working, other people also became mentors to me. One of them was a colleague in his late sixties. He dropped by my apartment every morning and we walked to work together. On the way, he would discuss sports and politics and, most of all, business. What he was really doing was teaching me lessons that he thought were important. He was smart enough to know that he had to tell me these things in a low-key, off-hand way that would be easy for me to accept. He figured out exactly how to do it. He was extraordinary.

Another man who was tremendously helpful to me was my supervisor, who was twenty-four years my senior. After work, we'd walk uptown together. For four years, we walked about fifty blocks in good weather and in bad. Occasionally we'd stop for a cup of coffee or a drink, and every step of the way he was talking to me about leadership, about literature, about all kinds things he thought I should know. Not everything filtered through. But a lot did, and I owe him for that. He understood precisely what he was trying to do, and he was very helpful to me. I've never forgotten his generosity.

Thanks to those experiences, I know how important it can be for a young person to have an older mentor. When a young person comes to me, either formally or informally, for guidance, I remember what I learned from the people who were my mentors, and I try to pass it on.

At the same time, my days of being mentored are not over. I think it's important to be mentored by people who are older, younger, and in entirely different fields. If you're entering a new business or beginning a new job, an older mentor—or in any case, a more experienced one—can show you the ropes.

But an older mentor is unlikely to have a handle on the younger generation. That's why I recommend having a younger mentor—and the older you are, the younger your mentor should be. A younger mentor can give you insight into what's hot, what's happening, how business operates today, how young people think.

Fortunately, it's not difficult to find a younger mentor. Here are a few ways to do it:

Look for someone at work. Keep in mind that you don't have to announce that you want that person to be a mentor. In fact, it's best not to, especially if the person is significantly younger than you: It sounds too intimidating. But you can certainly find someone to ask for advice or opinions, and I think that's a smart thing to do.

From time to time I eat lunch with a younger man who works in my building. We'll pick up a couple of hotdogs from a vendor and sit together on a bench. I don't ask him how to run my business. But over the years, he's given me a lot of insight into how younger people think, and that has been very helpful.

Take a night class at a college or university, and look for a young professor—or another adult student—with whom you might be able to connect.

Work with a trainer. That might mean a career coach. But it could also mean a physical trainer, someone who can talk to you in an out-of-the-box way while you're on the treadmill. It's a given that not all of those well-muscled young people are up to the job of advising, in which case you shouldn't bother. But quite a few of them are. I've been surprised recently by the number of people who have quoted their trainers to me. It made me think about the nature of being a mentor. What does it require, really? Sometimes all a mentor needs to be is a sounding board with a sensible mind and the ability to motivate, which is precisely what trainers do for a living.

Join a group that includes younger people, and seek them out. I have made it a habit to extend myself to the Public Relations Society of America and the International Association of Business Communicators as a speaker or program participant, partly because it's an easy way to meet the younger people in my profession. I don't want to become a dinosaur in my own field. Hearing their ideas, watching their responses, and talking with them helps keep me current.

And I may be wrong, but I think they enjoy sharing their thoughts with someone as obviously senior as myself.

Being a Mentor

Finding someone to mentor is easy. Anyone who seeks your advice is an automatic candidate. But you have to approach the relationship carefully.

Ever try to cram information down someone's throat? Ever try to convince a young person who is inexperienced in precisely the area of your greatest expertise that his or her goals are unreachable? Then you know how difficult mentoring can be.

To be an effective mentor, it helps to follow these principles:

- Don't be authoritarian. Rule number one.
- Have something to say, and keep it short. It's best to think in terms of headlines when you're mentoring somebody. Let them come to you for the details.
- Be informal. My mentors walked me up the street and down the street. We talked over coffee. Our encounters were never a big deal. By making them formal or uptight, by delivering facts and lessons, you risk turning a mentoring session into an uncomfortable tutorial. And no one wants that.
- Do not give orders. Do not say, this is the way it's done. No one likes to be told what to do, but young people are especially adverse to it.
- Don't take slights personally. When an uncomfortable topic comes up, young people are likely to push back or close down the discussion, sometimes in ways that hurt your feelings. Don't let it.
- Tell stories. You've got to jolly people along when you're mentoring. One way to do that is through telling stories. That way you can make your point, even about the most difficult

personal issues, without being confrontational. Sometimes it helps to be oblique.

- Always use humor.
- Be lavish with praise. Give people full credit for every contribution they make, however minor. It's the best way to keep the discussion alive.
- Despite repeated opportunities, never say, *I told you so.*
- Remember that younger people don't share your attitudes, even about mentoring. In *Generations at Work,* authors Ron Zemke, Claire Raines, and Bob Filipczak explore those differences. "Boomers," they write, "like mentors because they think it will them put on the promotional fast track. Xers like mentors because they are a kind of surrogate parent, someone who cares about them and will support them." It might be wise to keep those differences in mind, and act accordingly.
- Set boundaries. No matter how generous your intentions or how great the need, there's only so much you can do.

A Last Word

When I was young, I was sure of one thing: I did not want to lead a narrow, constricted life. Like every English major who has ever lived, I was affected by T. S. Eliot's great poem, "The Love Song of J. Alfred Prufrock." You remember him: he's the guy who measured out his life with coffee spoons and wondered, "Do I dare?"

I was determined not to turn into him. I wanted to have adventures, to take risks, to mingle with stimulating people, to see the world. And I have.

But I have become aware in the last few years that it's easy, as we get older, to pull back, to stop reaching out to new people or visiting new places or contemplating new ideas. I don't want that to happen to me.

I want my world to continue to expand. One way to make sure that happens is to maintain an open dialogue with the young.

10

Getting Back in the Game

Maybe you love your career but you've suffered a few setbacks. Maybe you decided, in one of those bleak moments that descend upon everyone once in a while, that your entire career has been a mistake and you should start all over again. Or maybe, after years of waiting for the proper moment, you've decided to dismiss your doubts and pursue your dream. Whatever your situation may be, it's not too late—it's never too late—to begin anew.

Yet these are troubled times. Millions of people in the United States are out of work and unemployment is approaching levels that we haven't experienced in generations. I've seen direct evidence of it. The Manhattan office of The Dilenschneider Group is on the same floor as Lee Hecht Harrison, an important outplacement firm. More than once in the months since September 11, I have gone to the washroom that we share and seen grown men literally bent over the sink crying because they have lost their jobs. It's a tragic situation.

Nor are we the only ones with economic troubles. With France and Germany facing similar problems, it doesn't look as if we'll climb out of this for a while. You would be foolish to consider a career change without acknowledging this reality.

Nonetheless, despite everything, I don't believe we're entering a dark age. I believe we're standing on the brink of the unknown, and we'll meet the challenge. As a people, we are inventive, alert, capable of finding opportunities even in the worst of times. I'm certain that in the years ahead, men and women around the world will come up with creative ideas and innovative products that will make life safer, easier, more fun. It's inevitable. The human spirit cannot resist the lure of invention.

Which is why, if I were contemplating a career move, I would draw up my plans in as careful a way as possible and launch my ship.

Here are the eight basic rules for starting—or restarting—a career, no matter what your age is and no matter what's going on in the world.

Rule Number 1. Find a Focus . . . or Fake It

Wanting to create change is not enough. You need to know what you want to do, and you have to be able to articulate it with some degree of specificity. For many people, this is not a problem. They know exactly what they want to do and they're passionate about it.

But a surprising number of people, for one reason or another, don't have a clue. They would love to commit themselves to a career, if only they could figure out what it should be. But every profession they can imagine has a downside, and so they feel paralyzed.

If this dilemma is affecting your life, you might consider talking to a career counselor or reading one of the many books that address this issue. (The classic in this genre is probably Marsha Sinetar's *Do What You Love, The Money Will Follow: Discovering Your Right Livelihood.*)

Books can be enormously helpful. But ultimately, only you can make a decision. When in doubt, trust your intuition. Most of the time, it will tell you which path to choose.

But if you can't seem to access that inner knowing, if you're lost in a fog of confusion, and simply can't make up your mind, I have one simple piece of advice: Jump in. Choose. Flip a coin if you must. And then give your all to whatever your choice may be.

True, every new venture has its drawbacks, and you will undoubtedly suffer from them. But you're already suffering. Better to take action and see what happens than to sit around waiting for inspiration to strike. Besides, allowing yourself to wallow in uncertainty seldom leads to clarity. It is just another form of procrastination.

As former Beatle George Harrison sang (in a song I hadn't heard until after his death), "If you don't know where you're going, any road will get you there."

Rule Number 2. Be Resolved

Without absolute resolve, you're unlikely to get anywhere. Getting back into the game is a lot of work, and you're sure to take a few knocks along the way. If you're not committed, don't waste your time. You'll only disappoint yourself.

For instance, I know a talented woman in her fifties who has had half a dozen careers since she passed the half-century mark. She's been a caterer, a party planner, a realtor, and several other occupations. But because she lacks resolve, she's flitted from one area to another and her success has been limited. Her frustration and bitterness leak out into her social contacts. As a result, people don't particularly enjoy her company, and she feels—correctly— that she hasn't gotten back into the game.

I've met a lot of people like that. They throw themselves into their new careers with enthusiasm. They rent fabulous offices, send out announcements, and distribute their new business cards, with the snappy logos and memorable e-mail addresses, to everyone. But the first time they hit a glitch or a slow period, they lose their determination and give up. My advice: Don't do that. Find something to focus on and, having done that, be resolved.

Rule Number 3. Set a Goal

Perhaps the most important step is setting a goal. Not a vague, feel-good goal; not an unrealistically ambitious goal; but a doable, reachable, specific goal.

This process is not the same for a person over fifty as it is for a younger person. A thirty-year-old person who's floundering may feel like time is passing him by. In reality (as we now see), time's on his side.

Time's on your side too, but in a different way. Because you don't have a lot of it to waste, you're ready to use your time effectively. You know how pointless and counterproductive it would be to set goals that will take twenty years to achieve.

That's why I recommend fine-tuning your goal into something that you can reasonably expect to achieve in two or three years.

To do so, you may want to quantify your goal, as many experts recommend. How much money can you realistically expect to earn in any given period of time? How many articles can you hope to publish? How many new clients can you attract? Writing down the numbers will help you know where you're heading and when you can expect to get there.

Rule Number 4. Make a Plan

Once you have a focus and a goal, the next step is to develop a step-by-step plan of action. This plan, especially if it involves a foray into new territory, will not work out in the way you're imagining. Over time, it will mutate in unpredictable ways. Even so, you have to map it out and act on it.

Begin by generating a list of everything you will need to do to make your goal a reality. Once you've listed a couple of dozen actions, prioritize them. Estimate how long each one should take and set up a schedule, complete with dates. You may want to write up a formal business plan, if only because the discipline that requires will encourage you to think things through as realistically as possible.

Your plan tells you where you should be now, three months from now, and a year from now. It provides an overview. Once you have that, you're ready to begin the work-a-day efforts that can carry you from here to there.

Rule Number 5. Use To-Do Lists

Is there a successful person on the face of the earth who doesn't make lists? I've never met one. In addition to your plan of action, which takes the long view, I recommend two kinds of To-Do lists:

- A weekly list, with a maximum of three or four goals. The purpose of this list is to keep you focused. It should concentrate on the main activities that will get you closer to your goal. So keep it short. A list of 117 items cannot possibly keep you on track.
- A daily list. Want to get mired in minutiae? This is the place. But don't forget to look at your weekly list first and to prioritize.

Rule Number 6. Take Action

Writing something on a list, as everyone knows, is a far cry from actually doing it. At some point, you have to act. But what if you don't know where to begin?

I discussed this with Carol Kinsey Goman, Ph.D. She has been successful as a nightclub performer, a therapist, a writer, and a communications consultant. In that last capacity, she has addressed groups in nineteen different countries and worked with virtually every industry on the planet. She has a deep understanding of the issues involved in career change, and her comments were on the money:

> You know, people get paralyzed. They wonder, what if this isn't what I should be doing? But it doesn't matter if it's the wrong thing. It doesn't matter. Get out there and take a step. Go in some direction. I've always been a fan of energy, and I think that if you get into action, the energy will snowball. Just do something.

Rule Number 7. Let People Know You're Starting

No matter how remarkable your product or service may be, you'll never get a seat at the cabaret if people don't know what you're doing. To launch your business successfully, you need to inform people in as many ways as possible. Have you compiled a mailing list of prospects and people who will recommend prospects? Have you sent out an announcement? Have you put out a press release in the local paper? Have you given a talk at your local service club?

Maybe that sounds like a waste of effort. Yet that's how Carol Kinsey Goman kick-started her career as a therapist:

> When I opened my business, I was divorced and broke, and I thought, no one will know I'm here. I don't have any money to advertise, the Yellow Pages have already been printed, and there is no way on earth that people are going to know that this office is open. So I thought, I'll speak to the Kiwanis and the Rotary Club and the Lions Club and any other luncheon group that brings in free speakers, just to let them know I'm here.
>
> I was working with hypnosis and doing a lot of work with athletes, and I thought that might interest men because I could talk about golf. I was also doing non-smoking and weight control, and I decided that would make a good luncheon speech. So I began to attract clients. One thing led to another, and my therapy practice took off.

Rule Number 8. Celebrate

You'll know you're making progress when you start passing milestones. Those milestones might be: developing a business plan, having a productive conversation with an influential person, getting a new client, signing a lease, publishing an article, giving a speech . . . you name it. Only you can decide which events qualify as milestones.

And only you can decide how best to celebrate them. I cannot emphasize enough how essential this part of the plan is. When you pass a milestone, seize the moment! You should say to yourself, I've done something important, I've fulfilled a goal, and it's time to celebrate.

Do something that makes you feel good. Go to dinner. Get together with a friend. Treat yourself to a book you've been wanting to read. If the milestone is relatively insignificant, acknowledge it in an appropriately small way. (I know a consultant who celebrates minor triumphs by sitting down at the piano and playing a Strauss waltz.) If the milestone is a major one, pull out the stops.

I know a fellow in South Florida who rewards himself when he reaches a goal by taking a dozen of his friends to a Chinese restaurant. At the start of the meal, he stands up and announces that he has succeeded against all odds and has called his friends together to celebrate with him. He has fun at these dinners but more important, they reinforce the accomplishment, which is the purpose of the celebration.

Asking for Help: The Don'ts

Most people are afraid of feeling foolish, afraid of being rejected, and too insecure to admit their weaknesses and ask for assistance. So they don't get the help they need.

But almost everybody is willing to assist if they're asked in the right way and at the right time. As someone who gives advice for a living and thoroughly enjoys the process, I can tell you that being asked in a sincere way feels good. I'm thrilled when I can make a positive difference in someone's life. When that happens, I feel validated as a human being—and I believe that most people feel the same way. If you understand that, you can tap into the experience of accomplished people and find precisely the help you need.

Unfortunately, many people don't know how to ask for help effectively, as I've had ample opportunity to learn. Here's how to avoid the most common mistakes:

Don't ask for something the other person cannot—or does not want— to give. In my case, I know a lot of powerful people. Many of them are my clients—my private clients. So you can imagine how uncomfortable I feel when folks I barely know ask if I can introduce them to those accomplished, busy people. Believe me, requests like that don't make me want to help. They make me want to sneak out of the room.

Don't ask for too much. Keep your requests reasonable. I'm thinking of one man who has asked me for help—on more than one occasion, I might add—by saying that he'd like me to give him advice, to give him business leads, to introduce him to people and, worst of all, to critique his work. To be blunt, that's baloney! It's a lot of work for me with no payoff in sight. That's not the kind of help I want to deliver, and I don't think I'm unique that way. When you ask for help, you want to make sure the person doesn't feel you're going to be a burden.

Don't ask for an overview of the field. Like many people, I'm not a fan of informational interviews. Aside from the fact that they are time-consuming, there is something disingenuous about them. I always suspect that, really, the people who request these interviews are hoping to be offered jobs. Since I know I'm bound to disappoint them, I'd just as soon avoid these interviews entirely. When I do agree to see someone as a courtesy, I give a pat presentation which surveys the field of public relations and public affairs in about seven or eight minutes. After that, there's nothing more to say.

Twenty or thirty years ago, these interviews may have served a purpose. Thanks to the internet, they no longer do. Don't ask someone else to do your homework. It's a turn-off. Plus, you don't want to waste a valuable contact by asking for something you can get easily on your own.

Don't ask in an arrogant way. This infuriates people. The underlying feeling is one of entitlement: "I deserve to have this information (or this money or this job). I shouldn't even have to ask." This is not a winning approach.

Don't beg. Presenting yourself in a pitiful way does not engender sympathy. It makes people cringe.

Don't ask for money. That's what banks (and parents) are for.

Don't ask for something that will require a huge investment of time.

Don't abuse someone else's personal time by asking for help at night, on the weekend, or on a holiday. Don't be an intrusion. Call at a time when it's convenient for them.

Don't push too hard. You need to apply some pressure, but tread lightly. You don't want the other person to dread the sound of your voice.

Asking for Help: The Social Contract

The key to asking for helping is giving the people you're asking the sense that helping you will benefit them. That can occur in many ways. They can benefit psychologically by feeling that they're doing a good deed. They can benefit because they're enlarging their network through you. They can even benefit monetarily.

A total stranger, someone who found my name through a professional association, once asked for my help, and I agreed to give it, gratis. He updated me daily on his job search, and I responded with tips, advice, analysis. Little did I know, though, that our dialogue would continue for about two years. Many times, I was sorry I'd signed on to this. But to my surprise, it ultimately paid off—for both of us. He got a great job and hired me as a consultant to his new employer. That was a tremendous reward.

Recently, a young man who had been referred by a top executive at *Reader's Digest* came to me for help. He impressed me because, unlike so many other people, he didn't just sit there, pleading. Instead, he had all kinds of ideas about how he could help me if I helped him. That made me want to help him more.

When you need help, think in terms of how you can benefit the people you ask. Otherwise, why should they bother?

How to Ask for Help

Here's how you can maximize your chances of getting the help you need:

Keep your request short, your approach business-like, and your demeanor upbeat.

Make the person you ask feel important. You don't want to be insincere or devious or sycophantic. But let's face it: Flattery works. If nothing else, you can say you're a person who is known for helping others. I appreciate that. I know that you've extended yourself to others many times, and people admire you for that. I need your help now.

Ask for something that's actionable—not just some data that you're going to write down in your palm pilot and stash away for all eternity. You want the other person to do something for you that will generate movement and lead to something else. You want to create linkage.

Ask for a contact or referral. You can say, Who can I talk to? If the person draws a blank (which rarely happens), rephrase the question. Ask, Is there anybody in this field who could help me take the next step? Is there someone who is knowledgeable about such-and-such? Sooner or later, if the person you're talking to is in the loop, he or she will pony up. Then you ask, What's the best way to contact that person? Can I use your name? Questions like that—specific and easy-to-answer—will produce results.

Let the person know that you intend to reciprocate. Even if it's the first time you've met, you can say, I've heard a lot about you. I hope that this is a relationship that goes on for many years, and I can tell you, I remember the people who have helped me and I intend to reciprocate.

It's possible that the people you say that to won't believe you. They may dismiss your words as a bravura performance. More likely, they'll admire your attitude (assuming you are sincere) and decide to help.

Let the person know that you need the help within a certain time frame. Say that you need the help in one week or two weeks or a month, and ask if you can check back in. If there's a specific opportunity in front of you, you might say that you need to act on it quickly. People are more likely to help you out when they have a sense of immediacy.

Offer assistance, especially if your request is a complicated one. Offer to draft the letter, to address the envelopes, to coordinate with the secretary, to make phone calls, to do whatever research is necessary, and so forth. Make it easy on the other person.

Say that you're missing only one more piece of the puzzle. It's discouraging to be asked to help when you know that dozens of things will have to happen before the goal is in sight. But it's hard to say no if the person asking is already most of the way there. People feel guilty saying no in an instance like that—a fact that you can use to your advantage.

Let the people you're asking know that you will spread the news. This is especially effective if you have friends in common. Everybody wants to have a positive image. Let them know that helping you will generate good publicity.

Nail the sale. Before you leave, say something like, What's the next step? Or, How do we begin? You should never leave the room without asking for the order. If you ask, the person has a hard time saying no.

What should you do if the person says, can we put this on hold? Sure, you say, We can. But there is a compelling reason why we should take action now. Without in any way projecting an image of desperation, be prepared with a convincing reason for making a move immediately. Never let a person off the hook too easily. After all, you're probably not going to have a second chance. You've got to succeed the first time you go to the plate.

Send thank you notes immediately. And as soon as you can, return the favor.

Who You Know

You've heard the old adage, it's not what you know, it's who you know. I'd like to dispute it. In all honesty, I cannot. I've seen too many examples of people who skim by on a modicum of talent shored up by a Rolodex of gargantuan proportions and a busy social schedule. The truth is that knowing the right people is enormously helpful. That's why, if you're hoping to change your life, you need to expand your circle. It isn't easy, though—especially if, like 50 percent of the population, you consider yourself shy.

By the time most people hit their fifties, they have conquered the worst aspects of their shyness. But high-stress events can bring those excruciating feelings back. That's what happened to a client of mine. She is a highly accomplished businesswoman who even gets invited to the White House from time to time. But it wasn't doing her much good, because whenever she got invited to an important event, she lost all her confidence and would find an excuse to back out.

For several month after I started working with her, I didn't understand why she behaved in such a self-destructive way. I wondered whether her inability to enjoy and take advantage of social occasions indicated a serious psychological weakness. Eventually I realized that it did not. The problem was simply insecurity.

I noticed that, like most people, she did fine once a conversation got going. The difficulty came when she had to initiate a conversation, particularly in a situation where she felt ill at ease—like the White House.

Fortunately, she was able to get a handle on her anxiety once she knew how to present herself (see Chapter 3) and how to start a conversation.

How to Start a Conversation

Large gatherings, whether they are professional conferences, charity balls, or PTA meetings, are an excellent way to meet people—in theory. In reality, breaking into established groups can be incredibly difficult.

I speak from experience. I'm not generally a shy person (you can't be in the business I'm in if you're shy), but I've had my moments nonetheless.

For instance, when I was in my thirties, I was invited to the Chicago Club for their "Renewal," an annual event, held the first Saturday in January, during which members gather around a groaning board laden with wild boar and roast turkey, to welcome the New Year. The members were influential people who were important to me in my business, and I was thrilled to be invited. Yet I felt overcome by a wave of awkwardness and discomfort. I dealt with it in the traditional way: I spent a lot of time hanging up my coat, a lot of time making sure that I looked okay, a lot of time chatting with the doorman. I didn't want to mix, and when I fi-nally tried to conquer my unexpected shyness, the club members were standing in tight circles and I couldn't break in.

I was wasting an opportunity. So I developed a bunch of ques-tions and forced myself to approach a few club members. Soon I found myself in the midst of conversations.

How can you start a conversation with a stranger? Eschew hard-ball questions. Avoid negative remarks. Keep your political opin-ions to yourself, at least for the moment. Above all, make it easy. Here's how:

- Look around. Get oriented. Get something to drink, alcoholic or otherwise. If you don't know anyone, approach someone who's alone and introduce yourself. Or join a group that has gathered into a loose, casual circle. (Avoid groups standing in physically tight circles because it will be hard to break into them.) After a few minutes, enter the conversation by re-sponding to a comment made by one of the other people in the group.

- Comment on the immediate environment. Better yet, ask a question about it. Doesn't the doorman Felix do a terrific job? And did you know that he's been here for twenty-five years? Isn't the food terrific? Isn't it wonderful to hear those Christmas carols? Phrase your question in a way that is likely to elicit a positive response.

- Ask about a local phenomenon such as the traffic, the weather, or—best of all—a local sports team. Are the Bears going to do the job this Sunday? How do you think the coach is doing? This technique generally fires up a conversation in about three seconds. If it does not, be prepared with a backup ques-tion. Worse comes to worst, you can revert to the perennial question: How do you know our hostess? Or . . .

- Comment on the news—but not on the front page. When you read the paper in the morning, find an obscure but intrigu-ing article, something on page sixteen that the other person is unlikely to have seen. If it relates to an interest you share (such as a professional or civic association to which you both belong), so much the better. Again, keep the tone of the conversation upbeat.

What if, despite all your efforts, you can't get a conversation off the ground? Or what if your fellow party-goer responds negatively to everything? What if he says that Felix is a moron, the food is inedible, Christmas is nothing but an exercise in excess, and the coach should be fired?

My first suggestion is to move on, because connecting with this person isn't going to be fun. Or you could stand your ground by saying that Felix is a nice guy; that the shrimp dumplings are delicious; and that yes, Christmas is often too commercialized, but this year it's different because . . .

Exchanges like these may sound dumb, but they work. They worked for me that long-ago day in the Chicago club. I fell into conversation with a much older man, who finally said, you're new here, let me introduce you around. My confidence zoomed. Later he proposed that I sit next to him at lunch. From that day on, my life in Chicago opened up, and I came to feel truly at home in the Windy City.

Hot Tip

The suggestions given above are easy ways to break the ice. But clearly there's more to be said on the subject. One expert who says it well is Susan RoAne. Her best-selling book *How to Work a Room: The Ultimate Guide to Savvy Socializing in Person and Online* tells you how to get into a conversation, how to get out of one, and more. I recommend it.

Looking Ahead

I have been accused of being a pessimist. I reject that view. I think I'm a realist. But be prepared: You may not like what I'm about to say.

Here it is: One of these days, you're going to look in the mirror and be appalled. Your health is going to falter. Terrible losses could afflict your personal life. Unexpected competition could kill your business. At some point, like it or not, you may even have to retire—and that, in my opinion, is never a good thing.

And then there's terrorism, global warming, and the state of the economy. In times like these, there is reason to worry.

Yet that's where people in their fifties and sixties (and beyond in many cases) have the edge. We're old enough to have developed perspective and coping skills. We long ago came to a recognition, however rueful, of both our abilities and our shortcomings. We are experienced enough to define our goals realistically, energetic enough to pursue them, and wise enough—or battered enough—to recognize the necessity of finding balance.

I think that's a privileged position to be in. And I think there's something exciting about being alive in uncertain times. I, for one, intend to approach the next phase of my life with the highest degree of creativity and commitment that I can muster. I know that any success I might have—and I'm defining success here in the broadest possible way—depends upon how willing I am to look ahead and take action.

Onward!

Several years ago, my mother had a chance to talk with my colleague Bob Stone, who is well into his eighties. "Bob," she said, "you must be getting ready to retire."

"No," he said. "I will never retire. Never."

And he never will. I intend to follow his example. I may not always be doing what I'm doing now. At some point, I'll probably look for a different intellectual challenge. I may try to reinvent myself in some way. But I can't imagine retiring.

In my opinion, nobody should retire. Okay, you might want to take a few months off while you're tooling up to do something new. You certainly might want to take a vacation. But retiring to play golf, perfect your bridge game, or catch up on old *New Yorkers* is giving up, and that's not a good thing.

In Chapter 1, I suggested making a list of everything you'd like to do in your life. For a young person, I wrote, putting 100 items on the list might be appropriate. For someone over fifty, it's realistic to cut that list in half. I think that's good advice. But I have to admit that even as I check off the items on my list, I keep adding more, both personal and professional. I suspect this process will never end.

One thing I know: I intend to make the next period of my life as fulfilling as possible. I assume you feel the same way. That's why I wrote this book. I hope it helps. And I hope that the next phase of your career brings you success, satisfaction, and joy.